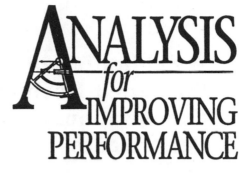

ANALYSIS for IMPROVING PERFORMANCE

A Publication in the Berrett-Koehler Organizational Performance Series

Richard A. Swanson &
Barbara L. Swanson,
Series Editors

ANALYSIS for IMPROVING PERFORMANCE

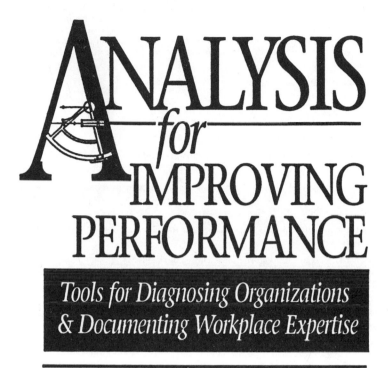

Tools for Diagnosing Organizations & Documenting Workplace Expertise

RICHARD A. SWANSON

Berrett-Koehler Publishers
San Francisco

Berrett-Koehler Publishers, Inc.
450 Sansome Street, Suite 1200
San Francisco, CA 94111–3320
Tel: 415–288–0260 Fax: 415–362–2512

ORDERING INFORMATION

Individual sales. Berrett-Koehler publications are available through most bookstores. They can also be ordered direct from Berrett-Koehler at the address above.

Quantity sales. Special discounts are available on quantity purchases by corporations, associations, and others. For details, contact the "Special Sales Department" at the Berrett-Koehler address above.

Orders for college textbook/course adoption use. Please contact Berrett-Koehler Publishers at the address above.

Orders by U.S. trade bookstores and wholesalers. Please contact Publishers Group West, 4065 Hollis Street, Box 8843, Emeryville, CA 94662. Tel: 510-658-3453; 1-800-788-3123. Fax: 510-658-1834.

Printed in the United States of America

 Printed on acid-free and recycled paper that is composed of 50% recovered fiber, including 10% postconsumer waste.

Poem on dedication page used by permission of William Arthur Ward.

Figure 13.3 on page 205 is from *Managing Strategic Change* by Noel Tichy (1983, p. 407). Copyright © 1983 by John Wiley & Sons, Inc. Reprinted by permission of John Wiley & Sons, Inc.

Library of Congress Cataloging-in-Publication Data

Swanson, Richard A., 1942–
    Analysis for improving performance : tools for diagnosing organizations & documenting workplace expertise / Richard A. Swanson. – 1st ed.
        p. cm.
    Includes bibliographical references and index.
    ISBN 1–881052–48–6 (hardcover : alk. paper)
    ISBN 1–57675–001–9 (paperback : alk. paper)
    1. Performance Standards.   2. Task analysis.   I. Title.
HD5549.5.P35S88   1994
658.3'14–dc20   94–13445
                                                          CIP

First Hardcover Printing: May 1994
First Paperback Printing: September 1996

    00   99   98   97   96   10   9   8   7   6   5   4   3   2   1

This paperback edition contains the complete text of the original hardcover edition.

Book Production: Pleasant Run Publishing Services
Composition: Classic Typography

To Walter G. Swanson
February 23, 1912–November 4, 1993

Blessed is the man
To whom his work is a pleasure,
By whom his friends are encouraged,
With whom all are comfortable,
In whom a clear conscience abides, and
Through whom his children see God.

—*William Arthur Ward*

Contents

Preface

The fundamental premise of *Analysis for Improving Performance* is that systematic and thorough workplace diagnosis and documentation provide the true basis for improving performance at the organizational, process, and worker levels. This is a book about mastering the work, not mastering the worker.

Organizational efforts at improving performance such as human resource development, quality improvement, reengineering, and performance technology are exhibited in various ways. One way clearly recognizes the organization's major business processes and their connectedness to core inputs and outputs for the purpose of adding value. Another, more prevalent approach is a pattern of independent activities taking place apart from the core organizational inputs and outputs and having no direct connection to business performance measures.

Regardless of the approach used, the standard performance improvement model includes five phases: analysis, design, development, implementation, and evaluation. It is how the *analysis phase* is carried out, however, that determines whether performance improvement efforts support *major business processes* or are simply a series of *activities*. Even though analysis practices are diverse, a fairly universal analysis vocabulary has developed. Almost everyone claims that the up-front analysis phase is important, even though professional practices leave much to be desired. Thus, the easy talk about analysis — at both the diagnosis-of-performance and documentation-of-expertise levels — can mean intense investigation to one person, or a fairly simple and routine activity to another.

My position, backed by research and experience, is that the analysis phase, and its requirements of organizational diagnosis and expertise documentation, is the most critical phase of the performance improvement process. It is also the phase that is most poorly managed.

Clearly, the activity-oriented view of human resource development, quality improvement, reengineering, and performance technology is driven by "feel-good" or "compliance" concerns, not performance. Program delivery — not performance — is primary. The activity-based view, with its emphasis on delivery, discounts the importance of the analysis phase. The activity-based view of analysis consists of superficial opinion surveys resulting in program popularity ratings, crude job descriptions, and inaccurate task inventories. Little, if anything, results in the way of substantive performance diagnosis and expertise documentation.

Overview of the Contents

Analysis for Improving Performance works on the assumption that performance improvement efforts, if they are going to add value to the organization, require an emphasis on the analysis phase — the content of the book. To meet these ends, I present practical tools in two major arenas: (1) diagnosis of performance and (2) documentation of expertise. *Diagnosis of performance* analyzes the performance variables (mission/goals, processes, motivation, capacity, and expertise) at the organizational, process, and individual performance levels. *Documentation of expertise* requires analysis of the work expertise needed to achieve optimal work performance. This analysis involves the components of job description, task inventories, and the detailed analysis of varying tasks: procedural, systems, and knowledge work tasks. Again, the fundamental premise of this book is that rigorous workplace diagnosis and documentation provide the true basis for improving performance.

At first glance, these tools may appear to be complex. In reality, they are easily learned and highly effective. The output of careful analysis is the critical information that accurately defines, frames, and guides effective performance improvement interventions.

Acknowledgments

A number of people and organizations have provided support for the research, development, and writing leading to this book. In the beginning, important research funds were made available by the Manville Corporation, with the full support of Gary R. Sisson and Gil Cullen, former executives of that firm. Additional organizations have provided support over the years. They include: CitiCorp, Kellogg Company, Onan Corporation, Northern States Power, 3M, and the University of Minnesota.

Important contributions to the ideas presented in the book have come from Deane B. Cradous, Gary R. Sisson, Barbara L. Swanson, and Richard J. Torraco.

The results of intellectual exchanges with David C. Bjorkquist, Gary M. Geroy, Ronald L. Jacobs, Joseph T. Martelli, Brian P. Murphy, Willis P. Norton, David L. Passmore, Steven Piersanti, Gene W. Poor, and Catherine M. Sleezer have also made their way into the pages of this book. I sincerely thank them all, because each has had a positive impact on my life and on the book.

St. Paul, Minnesota   RICHARD A. SWANSON
April 1994

PART ONE

ANALYSIS: THE KEY TO IMPROVING PERFORMANCE

Chapter 1

Linking Improvement Programs to Real Organizational Goals

As the role of performance improvement in organizations increasingly takes on strategic proportions through human resource development, quality improvement, reengineering, and performance technology, executives are being held more accountable in this arena. Their organizations spend millions of dollars each year on development efforts aimed at employees and customers. But while much is to be gained in terms of increased performance, money spent hastily on programs based on erroneous assumptions yields very little for the organizations and the individuals participating in them.

Performance improvement professionals often find themselves in awkward positions. They face many conflicting demands on their services. Everyone seems to have an opinion about the organization's development priorities. When executives attend conferences, they sometimes hear motivational speakers. Hooked by the fiery delivery and the bold promises of the management evangelists, the executives become enthusiastic about bringing the new messages home to their organizations and demand: "Buy the videotapes and see that everyone in headquarters goes through the program." Then, after a large

3

investment in time and money, everyone in the organization has the language of the consultant, but nothing else in the organization has substantively changed.

The performance improvement manager who dutifully responds to line management requests by charging out to hire an expert consultant eventually becomes committed to fulfilling the whims of decision makers. Instead, the performance improvement manager should be investigating business performance issues and offering sound proposals for development efforts that directly address important organizational goals. For example:

- What about that quality problem in the Armstrong division?
- Why are our engineers unable to integrate their CAD/CAM files with those of the customers' engineers?
- How can we reduce cycle time for our highest-demand product?
- Why can only two of our twelve financial investors regularly put together sound financial deals?

Each organization is unique. It has its own mission, strategies, and performance goals and challenges. By implication, faddish, one-size-fits-all performance improvement programs are not likely to fit any single organizational physique. With considerable confidence, I can say that in the short or in the long run, performance improvement efforts not connected to an important business goal will be seen as the ill-fitting garment they are and will be tossed out of the organization.

When Managers Decide to Follow Up

It is discouraging to discover how rarely managers provide support for participants following expensive personnel development programs (Fuchsberg, 1993). Managers have historically done little to ensure that the on-the-job performance of employees reflects what they have learned in organization-sponsored de-velopment programs (Parker, 1986). Meanwhile, the same man-agers say they want hard numbers about the contributions that development programs have made to organizational success. They say they would provide more support for development efforts if such evidence were made available (Kusy, 1986). When upper management does decide to follow performance improve-ment programs with evaluation, they often do not like what they find:

- The effort did not fill a current or future business need.
- The program did not fit the culture of the organization.
- The principles and systems covered in the programs did not reflect the expected work performance.
- Participants did not develop their expertise to the level of mastery required to perform on the job.
- Participants are punished by managers or peer groups for implementing new ideas and expertise back on the job.

There Is No Safe Haven for Performance Improvement Professionals

One Friday afternoon, a manufacturer of high-technology med-ical devices sent termination slips to twenty-six of the thirty members of its quality staff. For years, company insiders had casually discussed the quality function with a mixture of approval and disdain. In their eyes, the Quality Department had almost become an aloof operation seeing itself as a "College of Qual-ity" rather than a part of the business. Senior management had given the director of Quality a very loose rein and had allocated considerable resources to the department. The director subse-quently used the resources to provide employee and customer education that was marginally connected to the mission and strategy of the organization. The situation had reached the point where major surgery—amputation of the department—was seen by management as the only way to cure this economic drain on the organization.

Three Performance Questions
About Performance Improvement Outputs

Three simple performance questions, if they were asked at the outset of planning for improvement efforts, could radically change the role and contributions of the development functions in most organizations.

1. Will individuals perform better on the job after the intervention?

2. Will the process perform better after the intervention?

3. Will the organization perform better after the intervention?

All three questions focus on outputs. All three link development to the primary mission of the organization.

Top decision makers work hard at setting mission, strategy, and goals for the organization. Increasingly, performance improvement professionals are becoming members of this team. The aim, of course, is to maximize productivity and economic return by producing and delivering quality goods and services required by the customer. Managing the core enterprise of most organizations is subject to many uncertainties. The internal environment of the organization reflects the complexity and fluidity of its external environment. Within a context of changing culture, politics, and technologies (Tichy, 1983), management's decisions to invest in development efforts are too often made apart from the three questions about performance.

And performance improvement leaders, too, are often distracted from focusing on the organizational, process, and job performance questions. Two factors seem to be the source of the distractions that pull professionals away from their focus on performance. The first factor arises from management itself.

Many general managers know little or nothing about sound performance improvement practices, and yet they strongly attempt to control new efforts and processes. In the absence of a true understanding of the proper role of development, such managers let their personal agendas take over. The second factor arises from developers themselves. Many are ill-equipped to advocate or implement a systematic development process for responsibly connecting their contributions to the mission, strategies, and performance goals of their organizations. As a result, many development decisions are based, by default, on management's wants and preferences rather than on careful analyses of organizational, process, and individual performance issues.

Competent, responsible managers ought to be asking the organizational, process, and individual performance questions. Performance improvement managers can be equipped to provide the output data that will answer these questions affirmatively. Performance improvement efforts that are based on sound diagnosis and documentation work will almost always stand up to inquiry by organizational decision makers whenever they decide to ask any of the three performance questions—relating to organizational, process, or individual performance—or all three together. Development leaders ought to be able to show that their programs make a positive difference in their organizations in the form of improved performance.

Responsible performance improvement efforts are realized through an orderly process that starts with:

- Specifying an important performance goal.
- Specifying the underlying performance variables.
- Documenting the workplace expertise required of the performance goal.

The first steps comprise the analysis phase of the systematic performance improvement process, and they represent the scope of this book. The other phases address the design, development, implementation, and evaluation of the performance improvement effort. Because the analysis phase defines, frames, and directs the remaining steps, it is considered the most critical. Thus, learning how to diagnose organizational performance and document workplace expertise will pay off for both analysts and their organizations.

Analysis Work Is Important

The top executives of a major financial organization recently established a task force to evaluate its executive development center. They wanted to know if the programs the center offered were connected to the business plan. They also wanted to examine the quality of the center's individual programs. On investigation, it was found that the center's most popular offering was a program on "managing people" that had been in place for ten years. Over the years, several thousand managers had attended the program, and year after year, they had rated the program highly. But beyond the participants' personal satisfaction with the course, no substantial evidence could be found to support the idea that this expensive program had any positive impact on the organization. Further investigation showed that the program was severely lacking in content appropriate to the organization's philosophy of doing business or to the required day-to-day work expertise of its managers.

Most development and performance improvement programs based on the whims of organizational decision makers die out within two years. This ten-year-old program had become institutionalized. It provided busywork for a whole cadre of staff members and consultants. Regrettably, it took a major investigation to uncover a lack of purpose and content that should have been confronted when the program was first considered. The development staff, who had banked on the program's continuation into the distant future, had honed their presentation skills to a high art. Unfortunately, they were not prepared to perform the analysis required to connect the executive development function to the performance issues facing the organization.

Performance improvement professionals must be able to perform analysis work. They must be able to analyze performance at the organizational, process, and job levels and must know how to interpret the resulting requirement for workplace improvements before implementing development solutions. Their expertise and comfort levels increase by using specific diagnostic and documentation tools, thereby providing a solid foundation on which to build responsible performance solutions. The goal is to develop interventions that have an impact on individual, process, and/or organizational performance. The future of most performance improvement functions—and, for that matter, of our nation's economy—depends, at least in part, on managers and development professionals learning to work in partnership to achieve greater positive return from performance improvement activities (Swanson & Gradous, 1988). Careful analysis and follow-through are the means for accomplishing high performance returns.

Long-Term Success

The work of performance improvement professionals should be no different than that of other business leaders. The careful analytical processes that are expected and regularly performed in areas of strategic and tactical planning, product development, marketing, and systems engineering can also be applied to performance improvements. This book is devoted to systematic tools for diagnosing and documenting workplace performance and expertise. The content focal points of this book are displayed in Figure 1.1.

Conclusion

The case for engaging in front-end analysis is a practical one. It is the true connection to important performance gains, not the promise of performance. Analysis reduces the amount of perceived chaos in the organization through purposeful inquiry and personal expertise.

Chapter Two discusses the concepts of general systems theory as a foundation for thinking about improving performance in complex organizations. The remaining chapters provide the "real-world" knowledge, tools, examples, and exercises aimed at developing your competence in diagnosing and documenting workplace performance and work expertise—the keys to long-term professional and organizational success.

Figure 1.1. Analysis for Improving Performance Content Boundaries.

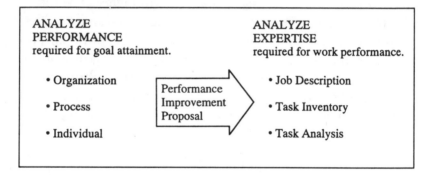

Chapter 2

Systems Thinking: The Foundation of Diagnosis and Documentation

Personal views about what drives organizations guides an analyst's fundamental thinking and approach to organizational problem identification and problem solving. Four single-dimension views will be discussed along with a more inclusive systems view. The systems view is one of perceiving organizations as complex, open systems.

Single-Dimension Views of Organizations

Some analysts view powerful leaders in organizations as the instruments for change—the *power-oriented view*. In power-driven organizations, managers assume that their job is to plan, organize, and control organizational processes. The performance improvement professional's role is to respond to line manager requests for activities and programs. Satisfying line managers is the major goal. Given this power view, developers serve at the beck and call of powerful organizational leaders and decision makers.

Some analysts view organizations as instruments for increasing the wealth of shareholders—the *economic view*. In economically driven organizations, managers assume that their job is to ensure high returns on all investments. Here the developer's role is to apply solutions that will yield high returns on investments. Increasing the quality or quantity of individual worker outputs is the major development goal. Given this economic view, performance improvement professionals adjust themselves to adhere to and assist in implementing the economic agenda of the organization.

Some analysts view organizations as machines in which the goal is obtaining the maximum quantity and quality of outputs through smoothly running, maximally efficient organizational processes—the *mechanistic view*. In mechanistic organizations, managers assume that their job is to ensure that organizational processes are highly efficient. The role for developers in this context is to respond to calls for improved work methods and for workers' adherence to ever-higher performance standards and goals. Given this mechanistic view, development is an important tool for improving the effectiveness and efficiency of established work processes.

Some analysts view organizations as social entities in which a high quality of work life is a major goal—the *humanistic view*. In humanistic organizations, managers assume that their job is to guarantee the high morale of workers, which will then logically lead to increased outputs of goods and services on the part of satisfied workers. Here developers' role is to assist managers and workers in building their interpersonal skills. Given this humanistic view, development is an important tool for improving the relationships between people up, down, and across the organizational hierarchy.

The above organizational views, whether applied singly or in combination, provide inadequate foundations for organizational problem solving. Holders of these limited views will tend to restrict themselves to a narrow set of problem situations and their solutions. They have limited what they will see or do as they work with managers and others on organizational change.

- The power-oriented analyst will tend to focus on political strategies — on pleasing top managers.

- The economically oriented analyst will tend to focus on strategies to optimize financial return on organizational investments.

- The mechanistically oriented analyst will tend to focus on strategies for getting more and more output per worker or process.

- The humanistically oriented analyst will tend to focus on creating harmony in the workplace and on making work life more pleasant.

The Systems View

Instead of the above four single-dimension views of organizational life, a fifth and more inclusive view is advocated. Many organizational development and performance improvement professionals have accepted the view of organizations as complex, open systems (Gradous, 1989; Jacobs, 1989; McLagan, 1989; Senge, 1990). Systems-oriented analysts assume that their job is to design and create high-performing organizations. In such a system, all the parts, or subsystems, work together to achieve the purpose of the whole organization. Developers work with managers in applying general systems principles to organizational problems and opportunities. Given this systems view, many tools for intervening wisely exist at the organizational mission, processes, and job performer level (Rummler & Brache, 1990). The analyst who takes a systems view will likely see the limitations of the other views of the organization. The systems thinker achieves strategic benefits by applying systems solutions to systems problems and opportunities. The systems-oriented developer will tend to focus on (1) defining the organization or system broadly enough to include the root cause of the performance issue and (2) identifying the primary source of the power to take advantage of a performance opportunity. At the same time, the analyst taking this approach will embrace the power, economic, mechanistic, and humanistic contributions to the performance problems, opportunities, and solutions.

Basic Systems Thinking

Systems theory was first applied by Ludwig von Bertalanffy (1968) to the field of biology and has since spread to influence a multitude of fields. Systems theorists believe that all configurations of things in the world should be viewed as wholes, rather than being taken apart and examined piece by piece. In systems such as the human mind, the human body, or the human organization, all the parts, or elements, affect each other in complicated and nonobvious ways. Studying the parts individually can disrupt their usual interactions so much that the isolated part will look and act very different from its normal pattern in its normal context. For this reason, it is extremely important to study the whole system at the same time one studies an element, or elements, of that system. Analysis work can be either the decomposition of a whole into its component parts or the piece-by-piece synthesis of component parts into a whole system. Both types of analysis work are important to performance improvement professionals.

All complex systems have certain properties in common, which make them appropriate for study (Clarke & Crossland, 1985). First, systems are assemblies of parts or elements that are connected in an *organized* way. That is, to focus on a single element and blame it for systems failure is counterproductive. All the elements in a system interact. Second, systems can be identified by their purpose. That is, a good way to identify the elements and interactions of a system of interest is to begin by identifying their collective output. Third, the elements of a system are affected by being in a system and are changed by being taken out of the system. That is, they stop doing whatever they were doing in the system whenever you remove them from the system. Fourth, systems do work. That is, complex systems exist to carry out a process of transforming inputs into outputs.

Fifth, systems have boundaries. That is, it is possible to set lines of demarcation to determine the elements included in a system of interest as well as those that are excluded. Finally, complex systems are open systems. That is, they are permeable so that forces in their environments, their contexts, will affect what goes on within the systems. In turn, open systems affect their contexts as they exchange energy, materials, and/or information with their environments. Even this simple portrayal of an organization as a system indicates that every organization has its environment and its inputs, processes, and outputs (Figure 2.1). Systems thinking demands that analysts understand the powerful influences that driving forces in the environment have on the organization-as-system and the challenges and opportunities these driving forces present to decision makers throughout the organization. The organizations that developers study are open systems; that is, they take in inputs—energy, materials, people, capital, and so on—from the environment. They then process these inputs and, in due time, return them to the environment in the form of outputs: goods and services.

Every organization has a purpose, a mission. The organization exists to carry out its mission, to do its work. *Improving the work life of the people in the organization is not, as some would have us believe, the primary purpose of a business organization. Producing quality outputs for customers is the primary reason for*

Figure 2.1. Simple Organizational System.

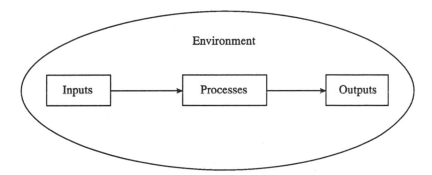

the existence of any business organization. When customers do not seek an organization's outputs, it must change what it does or die.

Every complex business organization consists of a number of subsystems, each of which has its own internal customers. They function interdependently with all the other subsystems in achieving the whole organization's mission. Subsystems, such as marketing, production, distribution, human resource development, and research and development, may be singled out by performance improvement specialists, depending on particular performance issues. Thus, what is treated as a system on one occasion may be treated as a subsystem on another occasion (Figure 2.2).

Figure 2.2. Interdependencies of Subsystem Inputs, Processes, and Outputs.

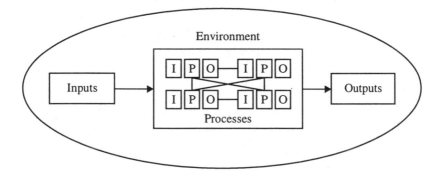

All such internal subsystems—each with its own inputs, processes, and outputs—can be identified by their purposes, their missions, and their customers within the total organizational scheme. Internal and external customers alike are powerful because they determine the quality, quantity, and timeliness criteria for their acceptance of systems and subsystems outputs. Decision makers within systems must heed the customers' criteria for the goodness of system outputs.

Power-oriented analysts tend to simply look to top management for problems to be fixed by means of their development solutions. Mechanistic and human relations developers focus on fixing individual employees and managers. Systems analysts, on the other hand, are aware that causes are often far removed from organizational effects. As a result, they feel compelled to struggle more with the breadth and the depth of the analysis.

These systems-oriented analysts know that focusing activities and programs on the wrong targets is a waste of organizational resources. They understand the importance of examining the interdependencies between organizational subsystems to identify the real sources of problems, most of which will not yield to isolated personnel development efforts.

Partial Solutions Don't Work

A software firm added new communications equipment to speed the process of answering customers who telephoned with software questions. Besides purchasing the equipment and training the product-support staff to use it, the economically oriented consultants offered training in listening skills and new methods for defusing the emotions of frustrated customers. As expected, responding to customers' needs took a little less time following the development program. However, increasing sales volume meant that the customer-support staff had to respond to an ever-increasing number of callers. They began hurrying each caller along. Rising customer complaints about the lack of response to their software problems prompted the vice president of sales to question the consultants about the effectiveness of their performance improvement effort.

As another example, the organizational development department of a large manufacturing company implemented a program to increase supervisors' expertise in conducting performance-based appraisal interviews. This activity was in direct response to a request from the management team. The driving force for the request was the company's president. While attending a professional conference, she had been persuaded of the urgent legal requirement to conduct unbiased performance appraisals. Simultaneously, the personnel department was carrying out management's directive to hire a consulting group to institute a new companywide compensation system. The two situations were treated as unrelated events in this company, even though the power-oriented human resource staff was aware of the potential effects of the new compensation system on the appraisals.

To take yet another example, an employee survey identified a wide-ranging requirement for increased communication skills in a rapidly growing service organization. Because their survey did not establish that the real organizational performance issues was intergroup communication, the performance improvement staff focused on developing interpersonal skills. The analysts failed to take a systems view of their growing organization and the requirement to assist increasing numbers of interdependent work groups in learning new ways to coordinate their work efforts. And the humanistically oriented staff, working at the interpersonal skills level, had completely missed a major systems issue.

Systematic Performance Improvement Interventions

In the performance improvement field, professionals place too much emphasis on creating new tools, methods, and techniques and not enough on the importance of integrating their use with the nature of the systems they are trying to improve. For example, the corporate person who attends any national professional conference will be offered a huge list of presenters, each claiming the merits of his or her new tool. What these presenters can't say is whether or not their new tool is appropriate for a specific organization, exactly where in the organization to apply it, and how to adapt it to the organization's needs. That is where systems thinking becomes useful. But it is easier said than done. Systems thinking consistently results in a struggle to define the elements of the system, the relationships between elements, and the framing of systems, or in the dilemma of where to draw the boundaries around a subsystem so it may be analyzed. While this effort is always a struggle and never perfect, these are not valid reasons for rejecting systems thinking.

In the end, it is clear to most people that systems theory, systematic performance diagnosis, and systematic documentation of expertise are powerful means for dealing with complex performance issues.

Systematic Performance Improvement Process

Most theorists and practitioners agree that a systematic process should be used to carry out performance improvement efforts. They also agree that a general performance improvement process consists of five phases: analysis, design, development, implementation, and evaluation. But practitioners and theorists do not agree on the detail and rigor required of the specific steps and subprocesses that make up each of the five phases. Therefore, I want to clearly state that I take a rigorous view of the performance improvement process.

Figure 2.3 shows the performance improvement process overlaid on the major elements of the organizational system. Again you see the core model of the organization within the environment. The environment is further delineated in terms of economic, political, and cultural forces surrounding the organization, while the organization is broken into mission and strategy, organizational structure, technology, and human resources (Tichy, 1983). Performance improvement is displayed as one process within the organization. The performance improvement process interacts with the other organizational processes — such things as marketing, production, distribution, and research and development.

Analysis is the first and most critical phase of the performance improvement process. In the analysis phase, developers and managers work together to achieve the critical steps of determining the performance requirements of the organization and the desired performance goal or standard. In this phase, developer and manager also work together to determine whether management

Figure 2.3. Systems Model of Performance Improvement:
Performance Improvement Phases.

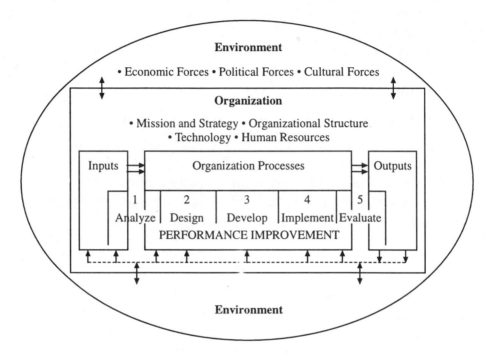

actions, development efforts, environmental forces, or some combination of these will effect the change in performance. In addition, determine precisely what people are required to know and
be able to do to perform in the workplace.

I divide the analysis phase into two parts, organizational
performance diagnosis and work expertise documentation (see
Figure 1.1). Performance diagnosis comes first. It is a problem-
defining method that takes into account the systemic nature
of the organization. It results in an accurate identification of
the actual and desired organization, process, or individual performances along with appropriate systems improvements to be
made by management and worker expertise that may need to
be developed. Work expertise documentation comes second. It
is a systematic method of analyzing and documenting the work

expertise — the detailed knowledge, skills, and attitudes required to perform on the job — as called for by the performance diagnosis.

Tools for executing the steps appropriate to diagnosing organization performance are described in Chapters Four to Seven. Tools for executing the steps appropriate to documenting workplace expertise are described in Chapters Eight to Thirteen. These latter steps include job description, task inventory, and task analysis. Task analysis defines precisely what a person is required to know and do in order to perform a particular task. Specific methods for analyzing procedural, systems, and knowledge work tasks are presented.

Beyond the analysis phase of performance improvement, the remaining phases include design, development, implementation, and evaluation. The linkage between all five phases is direct and substantive. The analysis phase, which must be completed first, defines and frames the entire performance improvement effort. The quality of the effort during the analysis phase is critical because it spills over into the substance of all the remaining phases. By contrast, the implementation phase only impacts the evaluation phase. Major errors can be made in any of the phases, but as you progress through the systematic development process, you encounter fewer opportunities to make serious process errors. What is more, errors in the later phases are less costly to repair. In contrast, a fatal error made in the analysis phase and discovered in the evaluation phase can be costly to rectify.

Conclusion

Managers of complex organizations face choices about improving performance and about the avenues they will pursue in achieving their performance goals. Instead of gaining a true understanding of the performance problems, they may crudely choose to hire and fire people or to streamline the process and fire the excess workers. Eventually, in even the most humane organizations, people with obsolete know-how are discharged to allow the hiring of people who seemingly have the capacity to perform in the present system or the ability to reshape the system. A systems-thinking person would judge these erratic organizational pulsings as ineffective and inefficient. As a positive response, the remainder of this book provides the tools to *systematically* diagnose and document workplace performance and expertise — the critical first steps in performance improvement.

Chapter 3

Case Study of Analysis for Performance Improvement

We know from the research on problem-solving behavior that good problem solvers control the definition of the problem. When they are confronted with well-defined problems, they quickly convert them into ill-defined problems with questions like "Why?" and "How do you know?" They efficiently collect relevant data and are able to synthesize it into an accurate problem definition and solution — independent of the predisposition of others. The personal traits of good problem solvers are intelligence, experience, and motivation.

Analysis for improving performance, and the tools presented in this book, are fashioned from expert problem solvers in organizational diagnosis and expertise documentation. To suggest that anyone can do this work would be foolhardy. Yet my experience has been that more have the capability than previously imagined.

The Acme, Inc. case is being presented at this point in the book to provide a common learning anchor. Throughout the book, examples relating to Acme, Inc. will be provided. In addition, numerous examples on other topics will be presented for the purposes of learning and generalization.

The following profile of Acme, Inc. is not intended to be complete. The case will unfold throughout the book. Rather, the following are pieces of a puzzle; each is interesting in itself, and together, they reveal a picture of Acme, Inc.*

Company Description

Acme, Inc. markets, designs, produces, sells, and distributes a line of replacement seat covers for automobiles. All the colors, patterns, sizes, and shapes of seat covers in the product line add to a total of about 130 options available to meet customer orders.

The Distribution Division has three departments: Order Handling, Shipping, and Inventory Control. Because of the complexity of the product line, the Distribution Division has its own data processing system to maintain inventories. About three and a half months ago, they installed a new inventory control terminal, and since then, the division has been experiencing numerous shipping problems. The organizational chart of the Distribution Division is shown in Figure 3.1.

Organizational Performance Records

A number of regular business measures are causing concern for the managers at Acme. The following run charts (Figures 3.2 to 3.4) on returned goods rates, inventory error rates, and shipper overtime provide indicators of serious performance problems. Review them and see what you think.

---

*Gary R. Sisson probably would rightfully claim to be the father of Acme. Sisson is president of Paradigm Corporation, Littleton, Colorado, and a superb performance improvement consultant. He has successfully used the theories and tools presented in this book year in and year out—an exceptional professional case study himself. I extend to him the following compliment: "When he enters an organization he never starts with a solution. He remains open as he questions and gathers information."

Figure 3.1. Acme Distribution Division.

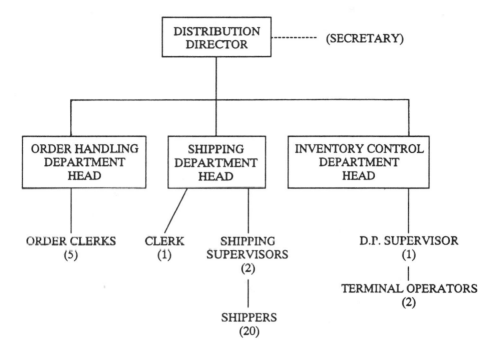

Your Role

You are a performance improvement specialist for Acme, Inc. You are relatively new with the corporation but have experienced a number of small successes in the Production Division during the past six months. This is the first time you have done any work with the Distribution Division. You also know very little about the shipping function. Even so, the plant manager is concerned and is expecting you to turn around a bad situation that appears to be getting worse.

Off-Hand Comments

As you have begun to move ahead on this important performance problem, snippets of information have come at you from a number of sources. It is all secondhand information or opinion. Some examples:

Figure 3.2. Returned Goods Rate.

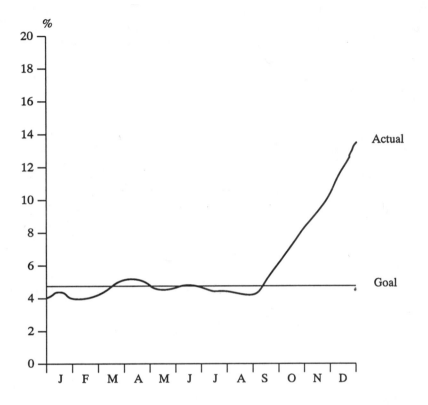

In the Order Handling Department

- A new streamlined system will be installed in six months. New computer terminals were installed three and a half months ago. One new and one experienced operator were trained by the vendor.

In the Inventory Control Department

- Computer terminal operators' overtime is too high.
- Inventory rates (actual count versus computer reports) are too high (see Figure 3.3).
- Fifteen percent of the computer reports are late.

Figure 3.3. Inventory Error Rate.

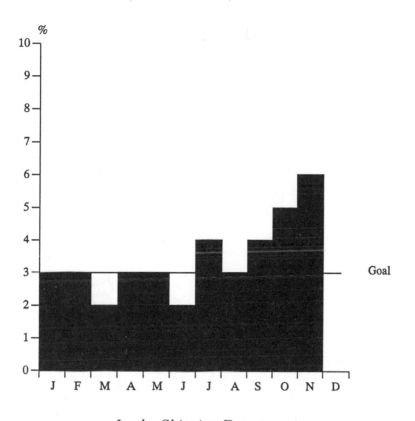

Goal

In the Shipping Department

- Shippers' overtime is too high (see Figure 3.4).
- Out-of-stock items are too frequent, as shown by the physical count.
- Shippers have no formal training and are trained on the job. Seven of the twenty shippers have less than six months experience.
- Shippers are ignoring lift-truck safety procedures.
- Returned goods are up over the past four months due to wrong product shipped (see Figure 3.2).
- Warehouse housekeeping is marginal to poor.

Figure 3.4. Shipper Overtime.

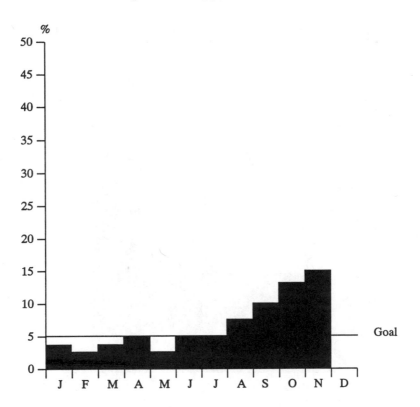

Interview Highlights

Six people in the Distribution Division have agreed to be interviewed by the performance improvement specialist as part of the investigation. They include the director of Distribution, head of Inventory Control, a terminal operator, head of shipping, a Shipping supervisor, and a shipper (see organizational chart, Figure 3.1). The highlights from the interview notes are as follows:

Director of Distribution

She acts powerful and talks in platitudes. She tends not to acknowledge problems and plays it close to the chest.

- The quality improvement director is blowing this situation out of proportion.
- Business cycles explain the performance records.
- Housekeeping in Shipping is a problem.
- The Order Handling Department may need help with their new streamlined system.

Head of Inventory Control

This manager doesn't get along with the head of Shipping and is 100 percent convinced there is a problem and that it is Shipping's fault. The jobs here are simple.

- Shipping is entirely to blame for the problems. The head of Inventory Control is always correcting their reporting errors.
- Terminal operators are tops.
- Shippers don't know the codes.
- The Shipping manager won't take responsibility for the problem.
- Overtime is up because terminal operators spend too much time correcting Shipping's errors.

Terminal Operator

She has been on the job for four years and thinks the present computer system is great. She is trying to do her job and is concerned about problems with Shipping.

- She is trained and knows the system.
- Three or four months ago, all kinds of bad reports started coming out of Shipping; she doesn't know why.
- Shippers fill out a ticket for each order indicating product codes and numbers of items shipped. Terminal operators get them and enter them. The computer keeps the running inventory.

Head of Shipping

This manager is catching flak from the head of Inventory Control and is really tired of it. He thinks he is being set up, since he is 100 percent sure his shippers are well qualified. Everyone is overworked.

- There are only two supervisors and one (Harry) has been out for three and a half months because of a heart attack. The Shipping manager can't get approval for a replacement. Normally, Bill works the floor and Harry works the office.
- Data Processing is screwing up the reports. We send them over and they foul them up.
- Data Processing doesn't know how to use their new system and their reports end up going to production, we get the wrong parts, and then we have to make substitutions. It's crazy!
- Shippers are good; a solid system of on-the-job training is in place.

Shipping Supervisor

The remaining Shipping supervisor (Bill) is hassled and overworked; he wants to get back to the warehouse as soon as possible.

- Bill has been going crazy ever since Harry got sick.
- He hates paperwork—Harry loves it!
- The clerk is now doing the paperwork and all Bill is doing is running back and forth.
- The training is good—old-timers teach the new people.
- Bill is best at working on the floor supervising the shippers and seeing to it that the trucks get off on schedule.
- He can't do the job of two people.

Shipper

The shipper has ten years experience and liked the job until Harry got sick.

- It has been a real problem since Harry got sick.

- Harry is the only one who knows the codes for the reports — he filled them all out.

- Bill won't fill out the reports — we do our best, but nobody ever trained us to do it.

- Everything is screwed up. The shipper goes to a bin, finds it empty, makes a substitution, and the customer sends it back. What a mess.

Interview with Shipping Supervisor on Teamwork

You are thinking of proposing a shipper program to train twenty shippers on teamwork, among other tasks, to make seat cover substitutions. As one source of data, the Acme performance specialist (PS) interviews a shipping supervisor (SS) expert in teamwork from the Acme Ohio operation. The transcript follows:

> PS: Thanks for meeting with me. Based on the new Shipper Job Description and Task Inventory you helped develop, we are moving ahead with a training program to prepare the shippers to work in teams of two to make seat cover substitutions. Your experience in team problem solving in Ohio has been invaluable to us.
>
> SS: Yeah, there really isn't any one right answer to substitution decisions. The best overall solution we have right now is that "two heads are better than one"!
>
> PS: Tell me more about the idea that "there isn't any right substitution."
>
> SS: Well, as you can imagine, the best decision is to have the exact item the customer wants. If we don't have

that, we're already beyond the "right solution." We're hoping all the other changes we're doing, including training, will radically cut back on the number of substitutions. We also are realistic enough to know that there will always be some substitutions. So, our big concern is to make the most reasonable substitute. We don't want to do anything dumb — you know, that will just cause more problems than it solves.

PS: What do you mean by "cause more problems"?

SS: Substitution is just a lot of common sense, but it gets complicated. If the order is for a conservative color and we're out of that, you don't send a bright red substitute. If you're dealing with a low-end customer, don't substitute with a high-end product. But if the only thing we have that will work is a high-end product and you get clearance to ship the high-end product to the low-end customer at the low-end cost — go for it.

SS: You know, these shippers have apparently been working day in and day out without talking to each other. That's the way it used to be here in Ohio. I'd bet anything that your people have what it takes to do an excellent job and to make reasonable seat cover substitutions.

PS: Well then, what is it they need from training?

SS: We've talked before about this and you've seen some of it firsthand. The key is to (1) make it clear that making seat cover substitutions is their job, (2) give them some uncomplicated training on a simple problem-solving method that requires them to work in pairs, and (3) see that they follow through on the job.

PS: Is that it?

SS: Sounds simple, I know. In some ways it is. The hardest part will be with your supervisors. They need training on how to keep their hands off the shippers' work and how to coach people without turning them off. I guess we'll be meeting with the corporate trainer on that topic after lunch.

PS: I see that you have some work backed up as a result of this time we had. Thanks for your trouble! You've been a big help. See you after lunch.

Conclusion

Clearly there are performance problems at Acme, Inc. While much more information is needed, the history of backbiting among the top managers must be having a large negative effect on the organizational, process, and individual performances. Even so, a performance analyst must be struck by the sudden negative performance indicators at the time when a number of corporate events took place. This looks like something that could be easily addressed.

The Acme case will continue to unfold throughout the book. As each phase of diagnosing organizations and documenting workplace expertise is presented, detailed analysis work from Acme will be presented.

PART TWO

DIAGNOSING
ORGANIZATIONAL
PERFORMANCE

Chapter 4

Concepts for Diagnosing Performance

"You know it when you see it!" can be said about a smooth-running organization — or an inefficient one. It is amazing how quickly an outsider, on entering an organization, can tell you that this place is or is not functioning well. Even so, the mere detection that the ship isn't moving or that the crew is on the edge of mutiny doesn't qualify a person as a performance diagnostician.

In a single day recently, I had the experience of being a consumer of services provided by an automobile repair organization and a health care organization. Within minutes of encountering each organization, I was blasted with messages. The automobile repair station, along an interstate highway, was staffed with personnel that treated me courteously, wore clean uniforms, had a professional manner, and relied on a sophisticated technological backup system. The health care organization I visited later that day could have learned a great deal from the repair station. The egotism of the staff, combined with their poor work systems and inept communication, hit me soon after entering the door. But, analysis at this level does not represent performance diagnosis and will do little or nothing to improve the situation.

Performance diagnosis is much more. It is (1) a problem-defining method that results in an accurate identification of the actual and desired organizational, process, and individual performance levels, and (2) the specification of interventions to improve this performance. Performance diagnosis is not casual work. It requires intellect, experience, and effort. Clearly, bright people with a great deal of experience are the best diagnosticians. Since few of us are naturally equipped for this work, we need tools that can facilitate the diagnostic process and direct the energy required of the effort. These tools help less experienced professionals succeed and experienced diagnosticians become more efficient.

From a systems perspective, it does not make sense to think about isolated snapshots of performance. For example, I have seen managers set "new" performance goals that were lower than existing goals without even being aware of their backward move. Also, I have seen personnel development activities focused on narrowly conceived and trivial performance when the same organization was experiencing crippling inefficiencies resulting from the lack of basic work expertise among large segments of its workforce. Even worse, I regularly see managers with a solution in search of a problem. This is what management cynics refer to as the "flavor-of-the-month" approach to performance improvement, often based on management fads.

Accurate performance diagnosis is the first step in improving performance. The research has consistently shown that individual, process, and organizational performance improves through responsible and systematic performance improvement efforts (Campbell, Campbell, & Associates, 1988). Proper diagnosis of performance examines key performance variables (mission/goals, system design, capacity, motivation, and/or expertise) at three distinct levels (organization, process, and individual). Only then can appropriate interventions for performance improvement be prescribed.

The performance diagnosis should result in: (1) a formal proposal to management overviewing the situation, the proposed intervention, and the criteria for success; (2) specification of performance at the current and desired levels of attainment; (3) a specific performance improvement intervention for a specific audience; and (4) management's commitment to the intervention.

Performance Diagnosis Concepts

A number of concepts direct the work of diagnosing performance in organizations, though the precise conceptual relationships will vary for each situation. At first glance, the time taken to consciously review these concepts may appear to be a confirmation of obvious information. But my experience has shown that what is obvious to one person may not be obvious to another. Thus, reviewing these concepts will reinforce the theoretical model for understanding and directing performance analyses.

Framing the Performance Diagnosis

The performance diagnostician frames the situation to determine the causes of perceived performance problems. At the start, neither analyst nor managers will probably have an accurate frame. For example, some managers will greet the analyst with, "Help! I don't know what's going on; everything is all messed up." Other managers will confidently assure the analyst that "first-line supervisors in the Accounting Department need timely information for decision making." Caution is required. The fact that a problem is clearly stated does not mean that the statement is accurate. *Both diagnostician and managers should resist the temptation to frame the performance situation too early in the process.*

As part of the diagnostic process, the analyst checks, rechecks, and adjusts the boundaries of the frame to include relevant elements of the organizational system. Approaching a performance analysis with a frame that is too large or too small can be troublesome. Setting boundaries that are too broad can result in inefficiencies in collecting excessive amounts of data. Setting too-narrow boundaries can result in ineffectiveness because inadequate data are collected. The cautious analyst checks and rechecks by asking:

- "Am I using too small a frame?" Probably, when the conclusions are too easily reached.

- "Am I using too large a frame?" Probably, when people intensely disagree about the performance issues being discussed.

- "Am I using an appropriate frame?" Probably, if the critical data from larger and smaller frames confirm the data from this frame. Probably, if more than one cause of an organizational, process, or individual performance problem has been identified.

A major concern is how to frame the organizational system so that the true causes of the performance problem are included in the frame. Even experienced performance improvement professionals will sometimes err in establishing the boundaries for a performance analysis. Performance improvement programs resulting fro n framing errors will generally be aimed at a symptom of the performance, not the performance itself. And even if the program appears well polished, it can prove to be ineffective and costly.

Characteristics of the Organization, Decision Makers, and Analyst

Threaded throughout the performance diagnosis process is the need to recognize and monitor the critical characteristics of the organization, the decision makers, and the analyst (Sleezer, 1991).

The distinguishing features of these critical characteristics that affect the performance diagnosis process are:

Organizational characteristics of the internal and external environment, systemwide components that impinge on the situation, organizational culture and politics, and the language used to influence behavior

Decision-maker characteristics including expectations, consensus among multiple decision makers, and their level of support for the performance improvement intervention

Analyst characteristics including diagnostic skill levels and information gathering biases (Sleezer, 1991, pp. 357–358)

Paying close attention to the characteristics of the organization, decision makers, and analyst during the diagnostic process is important in obtaining a *common perception* of the real performance problem and proper remedy. A paradox emerges, however, because a common perception can build from a smooth sales pitch as well as from a disciplined diagnostic process. In fact, support for implementing an activity can be gained even when the activity does not show much promise of improving performance. The emphasis on a substantive improvement in performance differentiates this book from theories and practices that are barely, if at all, connected to performance. For example:

Quality management: ISO 9000. This approach does not actually promise to improve quality. It offers documentation tools that have the potential to improve quality (DuPont, 1989).

Human resource development. The adult learning perspective of workplace education and training does not promise to improve organizational or worker performance. It promises worker knowledge with "the possibility of performance change or general growth of the individual" (Nadler & Nadler, 1990, p. xxvii).

Accelerated learning. Accelerated learning is an example of New Age learning methods that promise faster, better, cheaper, and more enjoyable learning backed up only by flimsy testimonials as supporting evidence (Center for Accelerated Learning, 1992). After reviewing the research on accelerated learning, one scholar concluded— let the buyer beware (Torraco, 1992).

Thus, the eager and well-intentioned manager agrees to invest in an intervention that is supposed to make things better. The true state of affairs is that many interventions do not deliver what they promise and can even hurt the performance of an organization. Piecemeal and unsystemic performance improvement interventions have the potential of disrupting operations more than improving them. At a minimum, they can waste resources in terms of direct and indirect costs.

Sometimes You Start in the Middle

In the next chapter, the organizational diagnosis process is presented as a flowchart. This suggests that you move from left to right and that there is a logical beginning, middle, and end. Theoretically this is the way it should be and *is* the way an expert diagnostician ends up laying it out in his or her mind, even though the starting point may be in the middle or the end.

The reality of the workplace is that the boss may confront you with any of the following starting points to a performance diagnosis:

- We don't have a problem.
- We think we have a problem. Can you help?
- Here is the problem. What is the solution?
- Here is the problem and here is the solution!

When the boss says "Here is the problem. What is the solution?" you are plunked right into the middle of the performance diagnosis process. While the boss is indicating that the problem has already been defined, the question of the accuracy of the definition comes up. It may be accurate, but as an expert investigator you pull back—ask a few questions, review available documents, and make some of your own observations to check it out. In doing this, you temporarily (and maybe privately) reject the problem as defined by the boss and quickly come up with your own conclusion, even if it is one that agrees with the boss, and then move on to determining an appropriate intervention. Through this loop the analyst retains the responsibility of defining the problem.

Conclusion

Performance diagnosis is a complex, multidimensional activity. Issuing a simple survey to gather managerial or employee opinions about development options may help build common perceptions but will rarely suffice in accurately defining performance issues or deficiencies in worker expertise. Diagnosing organizations for the purpose of improving performance requires a substantial investment, with the realistic potential of high gains.

To this end, the following three chapters organize and present the critical elements of diagnosing workplace performance.

Chapter 5

The Performance Diagnosis Process

Workplace performance diagnosis converts ill-defined symptoms of trouble into a well-defined performance problem and performance improvement proposal. Performance diagnosis is *not* the springboard of "knee-jerk management" or "sixty-second solutions." Sometimes it works out that way—a quick fix for solving an easy performance problem—but that is not the norm. Performance diagnosis is rigorous work that yields powerful solutions for the purpose of improving performance.

Performance Diagnosis

Performance diagnosis is a problem-defining method. It results in (1) an accurate identification of the actual *and* desired performances at the organizational, process, and/or individual levels, along with (2) the specification of interventions to improve performance. The general process of performance diagnosis contains five phases (Figure 5.1).

The process starts with articulating the initial purpose of the diagnosis. It then moves into three realms: performance variables, performance measures, and performance needs. These three phases are pursued concurrently and at rates dictated by

44

Figure 5.1. Diagnosing Performance.

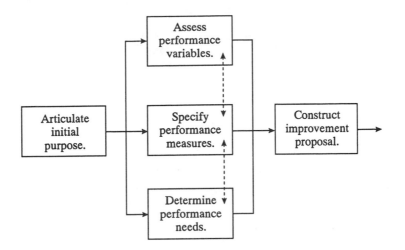

the situation. The performance diagnosis process culminates in a performance improvement proposal. This proposal acts as a synthesis of the findings and provides the springboard for organizational approval and action.

The following sections of this chapter detail the first four phases of the performance diagnosis process. The final organizational diagnosis phase—developing the performance improvement proposal—is presented in Chapter Six. The data collection activities that thread through all the analysis work are discussed in Chapter Seven.

Initial Purpose

It is important to start the workplace performance diagnosis process by articulating the original purpose of the diagnosis. The diagnostician does this by identifying four factors related to performance (Figure 5.2). Articulating the initial purpose of the performance diagnosis in this way guides the analyst through often vague and contradictory information.

Initial Indicators of the Performance Issue.   The initial indicators of a performance issue will most likely come from the

Figure 5.2. Articulating the Initial Purpose.

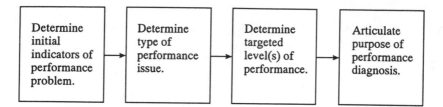

| Determine initial indicators of performance problem. | → | Determine type of performance issue. | → | Determine targeted level(s) of performance. | → | Articulate purpose of performance diagnosis. |

decision maker initiating the effort or the decision maker's agent. These indicators typically revolve around a critical event, a person, or a change in external conditions—production is down, there is a feeling of mutiny in the Research and Development Division, the president is not pleased with the amount of paper crossing everybody's desk, the V.P. of International is unhappy about how the work of his group fits into the organization, or technology is advancing too fast to keep up.

The initial indicators of performance reported by managers to the analyst may not match the stated type or level of performance they are *requesting*, however. For example, when 50 percent of the production product is waste or rework (indicator)—a present and serious performance problem—this is no time to be responding to a request for cross-training employees for the purpose of covering for each other on upcoming summer vacations. Sorting through the interviews, records, and on-site observations will surely point the diagnostician in the direction of a different problem than any deficiencies in cross-training.

Thus, it is important to sort out the early perceptions in the diagnosis process. Early perceptions are often strongly held and inaccurate. Your job as a diagnostician is to remain inquisitive and neutral. The utility of remaining open is that it expands your possibilities before you come to a conclusion. Creating a matrix in your head or on paper that helps you review the situation in terms of (1) type of performance issue and (2) level of performance encourages you to ask more questions and to think beyond the original felt need.

Type of Performance Issue. Classifying the performance issues into three categories helps separate the multidimensional
problems in an organization and assists you in articulating the
purpose of the organizational diagnosis. The three types of performance issues are: (1) present problems, (2) improvements (to
the present situation), and (3) future requirements (Swanson,
1982; Bjorkquist & Murphy, 1987).

This practical classification scheme is essentially respon-
sive to time. It acknowledges that while multiple performance
issues exist in any organization at any one time, there are also
multiple performance issues over time. *Present performance problems* revolve around performance outputs that are expected and
planned for but that are not being reached. This type of performance problem causes pain in the organization, ineffectual
processes, and dejection in workers — missed goals and obvious
low performance. The conditions are ripe for large performance
gains or high performance improvement potential (Gilbert, 1978).
The conditions are also ripe for blaming and secrecy. The initial data sources for present performance problems tend to be
basic business measures that stare you in the face: regular company performance records (Swanson, 1989).

Improvements and future requirements do not carry the
same intensity as present problems. They are generally more
subtle and may possibly be pursued at a more leisurely pace.
The initial data sources for improvements and future requirements tend to be employee and customer surveys: questionnaires
or interviews.

Without a sense of crisis, *performance improvement* issues
in an established organization, process, or individual tend to be
more rational and incremental. Also, this approach to performance tends to attract more internal experts with cooperative
mindsets than is true with the other two types of performance
issues. Quality improvement projects regularly identify opportunities for performance improvements.

Future performance requirements present another twist to
the situation we've just been discussing. Sometimes future re-

quirements are similar to improvements to an existing system, just set off into the future. For example, a new decision-making process or production system will be installed twelve months from now. Installing these well-defined systems in an already smooth-running operation can involve a fairly straightforward performance improvement task, though it may require a great deal of effort. Even so, the future time frame must be considered, since conditions will almost certainly be different later. A more unsettling situation is preparing for a radically new future and/or an undefined future. An example is the reengineering of major organizational processes going on in many firms today. Can you imagine attempting to determine the high-tech education and training needs of a sophisticated workforce based on technology that does not yet exist? This level of uncertainty creates extreme tension. In these conditions, even with the most systematic reengineering approach, unique forces are at work as leaders struggle with conflicting views of the future. And certain important variables should be taken into account. In particular, the role, status, personality, and experience characteristics of organizational experts providing diagnostic information for future requirements should be heeded. *Role* can include specialized knowledge versus project planning; *status* may entail on the way up versus on the way out; *personalities* can be strong and vocal versus weak and nonvocal; and *experience* could involve high versus low experience with technology (Swanson, 1982).

Targeted Levels of Performance.   Another arena of perceptions that should be considered in articulating the purpose of the diagnosis involves levels of performance. Three levels are identified and consistently referred to throughout the discussion of the remaining performance diagnosis phases:

- Organizational
- Process
- Individual (job/performer)

These three levels have been carefully presented by Rummler and Brache (1990), who describe each as follows: The *organizational level* "emphasizes the organization's relationship with its market and the basic 'skeleton' of the major functions that comprise the organization" (p. 15). For the *process level*, the analyst must go "beyond the cross functional boundaries that make up the organization chart [to] see the work flow—how the work gets done." At this level, "one must ensure that processes are installed to meet customer needs, that those processes work effectively and efficiently, and that the process goals and measures are driven by the customers' and the organizations' requirements" (p. 17). At the *individual level*, it is recognized that processes "are performed and managed by individuals doing various jobs" (p. 17).

System theory helps us understand the three levels. For example, the cause of a company sending a customer a contract bid containing an inaccurate budget and an incomplete list of services may lie in any or all three levels. Even so, the decision maker may be falsely convinced early on that the cause is lodged at a single level. For example: "There is so much bureaucracy around here that it is a miracle anything even gets done!" or "The financial computer program has a glitch in it!" or "Our financial analysts are incompetent!"

Articulated Purpose of the Performance Diagnosis. Remember the recent business records for Acme, Inc. presented in Chapter Three. The following *articulated purpose* notes the performance issue, the type of performance, and the targeted levels of performance for Acme:

> The purpose of this performance improvement effort is to reduce Acme, Inc.'s seat cover returns and employee overtime. This is a *present performance problem* having severe potential financial consequences to the company and its employees. At this point, it is difficult to determine the appropriate *level(s) of performance*— organizational, process, and/or individual—needing attention.

The articulated purpose of the performance diagnosis at the front end is followed by three phases—assessing performance needs, performance measures, and performance variables—that can be pursued simultaneously. The information and decisions for each of these steps need to be arrived at. Practical logistics will control the timing of the steps.

Returning to the general process of performance diagnosis (Figure 5.1), the articulated initial purpose leads to a concurrent examination of performance variables, performance measures, and performance needs.

Performance Variables

To assess *performance variables,* an investigation of the five performance variables at the three performance levels should take place. To assist in understanding the dynamics of the performance variables phase, I present a three-step process model in Figure 5.3.

The first step is to scan the available data on the performance variables and how they are presently operating. This requires the analyst to carry forward the existing knowledge of performance level(s), performance needs, and performance measures, and to scan these data for assessing the connections to the performance variables.

At this point, the diagnostician may have already determined that the performance problem is lodged at a particular performance level or combination of levels (organizational, process, and/or individual). The possible causes of performance

Figure 5.3. Assessing Performance Variables.

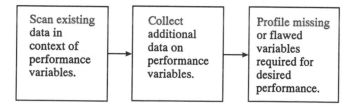

problems usually reside within one or more of five performance variables: mission/goals, systems design, capacity, motivation, and expertise (Sisson & Swanson, 1990).

These performance variables, matrixed with the levels of performance—organizational, process, and/or individual—provide a powerful perspective in diagnosing performance. For example, a work process may have a goal built into it that is in conflict with the mission and/or goal of the organization or of a person working in the process. The questions presented in the performance variable matrix help the diagnostician sort out the performance overlaps and disconnects (Figure 5.4).

A popular saying comes to mind: Pit a good performer against a bad system and the system will almost always win. How else to explain the failure of high-aptitude experts? When the work system ties the hands of competent persons behind their backs and then punishes them for doing their best, they either *quit and leave* or *quit and stay!* Likewise, when a well-designed work process is coupled with organizational policies and procedures that hire employees lacking the capacity to perform the work, no reasonable amount of training will get the employees up to required performance standards.

An investigation and comparison of each of the five performance variables at each of the three performance levels is required. Thus, a process could have a capacity that is less than the capacity of an individual working in it. Or the mission/goals of individuals can be out of sync with the goals of the process they work, and the process goals may have little connection to the overall organizational goals. Such performance disconnects must be identified.

The initial connections of performance levels (organizational, process, and/or individual) to performance variables (mission/goals, work system, capacity, motivation, and/or expertise) may be incomplete. The second step is the collection of additional data to complete or confirm the variables as they are functioning in the case under investigation. The third step in the process is to profile the missing or flawed variables for

Figure 5.4. Performance Diagnosis Matrix of Enabling Questions.

PERFORMANCE LEVELS

PERFORMANCE VARIABLES	Organizational Level	Process Level	Individual level
Mission/ Goal	Does the organizational mission/goal fit the reality of the economic, political, and cultural forces?	Do the process goals enable the organization to meet organizational and individual missions/goals?	Are the professional and personal mission/goals of individuals congruent with the organization's?
Systems Design	Does the organizational system provide structure and policies supporting the desired performance?	Are processes designed in such a way as to work as a system?	Does the individual design support performance?
Capacity	Does the organization have the leadership, capital, and infrastructure to achieve its mission/goals?	Does the process have the capacity to perform (quantity, quality, and timeliness)?	Does the individual have the mental, physical, and emotional capacity to perform?
Motivation	Do the policies, culture, and reward systems support the desired performance?	Does the process provide the information and human factors required to maintain it?	Does the individual want to perform no matter what?
Expertise	Does the organization establish and maintain selection and training policies and resources?	Does the process of developing expertise meet the changing demands of changing processes?	Does the individual have the knowledge, skills, and experience to perform?

performance improvement. In the Acme Shipping Department, for example, the following *profile* resulted:

> *Mission/goal.* Both the company and individuals clearly are concerned about surviving and prospering. While these common goals need to be harmonized, the individual "survival goals" seem to be predominant at this time and negatively affecting the company. This performance concern is being addressed by the Total Quality Management Proposal that has recently been endorsed by the president.
>
> *Systems design.* The department is seriously understaffed, with only one of two supervisors currently on the job. The second supervisor has been out for five months with a major illness and will not be returning to work. In addition, informally and over time, job roles and duties in Shipping have become redefined, reduced, and isolated.
>
> *Capacity.* Employees are underutilized. Most shippers have the aptitude to understand the shipping system and how to complete the shipping tickets.
>
> *Motivation.* Adversarial relationships between departments make it hard to admit limitations. Employees want to do a good job, yet are cautious about being made scapegoats.
>
> *Expertise.* Only the hospitalized supervisor has the expertise to complete order tickets. The shippers do not have a systems perspective of the company or their department. The legitimate seat cover substitution task occurs infrequently, is complex, and requires orderly problem-solving skills.

Performance Measures

To specify the *performance measures*, the relevant output units of performance at the organizational, process, and/or individual levels need to be identified. It is foolhardy to talk about development, change, and performance improvement without specifying the measure of performance. A target needs to exist. It may be as all inclusive as market share in a five-year period, or a narrower measure such as cash register errors in an eight-hour shift or the production of molded insulators per two-minute cycle. Without the target clearly in mind, it is almost impossible to think intelligently about appropriate performance improvement actions.

A process model may help to clarify the dynamics of the phase of performance diagnosis in which performance measures are specified; see Figure 5.5.

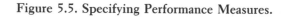

Figure 5.5. Specifying Performance Measures.

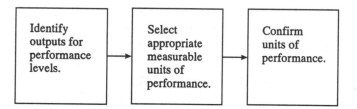

In specifying performance measures, the diagnostician needs to keep in mind (1) the levels-of-performance perspective (organizational, process, and individual), including the systems outputs at each level, and add (2) a units-of-performance perspective to the picture. The latter perspective provides a scheme for categorizing measures of performance. The scheme includes the following features:

- Time
- Quantity
- Quality (Swanson & Gradous, 1988; Swanson, 1992a)

The original notion of the workplace performance being analyzed is usually fuzzy and in need of clarification. For example, the original perception may be that too much time is spent in meetings. If confirmed, reducing the meeting time would be the appropriate performance measure. Additional investigation may reveal that important decisions need to be made that are not being made in a timely manner because of poorly run meetings. The output could then shift to the number of decisions or the quality features of company meetings.

Time is defined here as the measurable interval between two events or the period during which some activity occurs. In the workplace, performance is commonly measured in terms of time. Reductions in performance time usually yield important financial consequences to the organizations (Swanson & Gradous, 1988, p. 40).

Quantity is a measure of the exact amount or number of products, services, or other outcomes that result from worker or work-group performance. Quantity units are relatively easy to define and monitor in the workplace. Examples of such quantity units are the numbers of patents approved, clients served, sundaes sold, and sales earned. All three of the performance dimensions must be quantified, but the "quantity" dimension is the only one that is restricted to counting the simple, usually observable, worker or work-group outputs (Swanson & Gradous, 1988, p. 40).

Quality features are the characteristics of products or services that meet agreed-on specifications. Quality features of a product or service typically revolve around design, procurement, manufacturing, marketing, sales, service, customer education, and ultimate disposition (Tribus, 1985). Quality features can be measured and estimated in value.

The process of specifying performance measures within the performance diagnosis contains three steps (see Figure 5.5). The first step is to identify the systems outputs of performance for the three levels. The second step is to select the appropriate units of performance. The final step is to confirm the appropriateness of these units.

In Acme, Inc., the investigation resulted in units of performance along with the existing performance and desired output goal. They were as follows:

The performance goals for the Shipping Department in the next six months are to: (1) reduce Shipping overtime

by 10 percent, as measured by clock hours of overtime
and (2) reduce the inventory error rate by 3 percent, as
measured by individual order errors in relation to those
processed.

Returning to the general process of performance diagnosis (Figure 5.1), the examination of performance variables and performance measures is combined with an examination of performance needs.

Performance Needs

To help you understand the dynamics of the *performance needs* phase of the organizational diagnosis, I have included a process model consisting of three steps (Figure 5.6).

Figure 5.6. Determining Performance Needs.

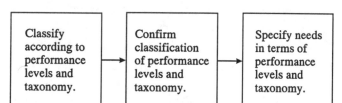

To determine performance needs, an investigation of the performance issue in terms of both performance level and performance taxonomy must take place. The discussion of levels (organizational process, and/or individual) earlier in this chapter needs to be recalled. Remember that each level sets out profoundly different perspectives. This, combined with the taxonomy of performance, allows a deeper understanding of the performance issue in question.

The taxonomy of performance lays out five tiers of performance: understand, operate, troubleshoot, improve, and invent (Figure 5.7). This taxonomy is divided into two general categories: *maintaining the system* and *changing the system*. Since almost all organizations have to do both and are struggling with both, they regularly get them mixed up. The result of undisciplined jumping from one tier to another can result in performance improvement schizophrenia. I consistently observe organizations delivering support and resources at one level and expecting performance at another level. This is done without realizing the built-in discrepancy between their performance interventions and performance expectations.

Figure 5.7. Taxonomy of Performance.

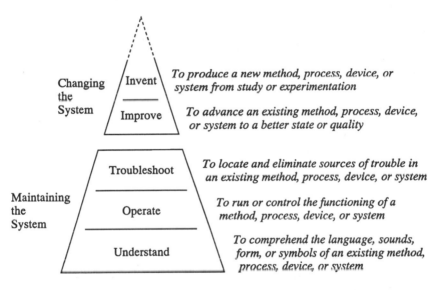

The performance taxonomy provides a lens that helps operationalize systems theory for those who work in complex organizations. For example, a quality improvement effort to "change the system" could hit a brick wall because there is no documentation of the expertise required to "maintain the existing system." Thus, moving from the performance concern of *change* to the prerequisite issue of how to *maintain* may be the critical step in getting to the concern for *change*.

While systems theorists assure us that business and industry conceptually operate as an open system — one that interfaces with other systems and is continually influenced by those systems

(Senge, 1990, 1993)—the practical organizational goal is to establish closed systems, as short-lived as they might be, for producing and delivering goods and services. These temporary, closed systems are mastered and *maintained* at the understanding, operational, and troubleshooting levels. The closed system is imperfect, and thus the *change* tiers of the taxonomy of performance (improve and invent) provide the added dimensions to sort out the full range of possible performance issues facing the diagnostician.

At the simplest level, it is no surprise to the experienced diagnostician that organizations that value, establish, and reward people for following rules have a hard time involving them in changing the system. Also, individuals who are trained to simply follow operational steps end up not understanding the system in which they operate and are not able to troubleshoot those systems, let alone improve them or invent new systems.

Thus, the first step in determining performance needs (see Figure 5.6) is to classify the problem by performance level (organizational, process, and/or individual) and then provide an initial judgment as to the performance taxonomy tiers (understand, operate, troubleshoot, improve, and invent).

These estimates of performance levels (organizational, process, and/or individual) connected to performance taxonomy (understand, operate, troubleshoot, improve, and invent) must be confirmed by data and people as these data are fed back into the diagnostic process. Once confirmed, the diagnostician can specify the needs in terms of levels of performance and taxonomy tiers. In Acme, Inc., for example, this information resulted in the following specification of *performance needs*.

> The company has been experiencing a number of disturbing and costly performance indicators over the past four months. Included are a 7 percent increase in returned goods (from 5 percent to 12 percent), a 3 percent increase in inventory error rate (from 3 percent to 6 percent), and a 10 percent increase in shipper overtime (from 5 percent to 15 percent). All three levels of performance of the shipping function—organizational, process,

and individual—will require attention. The organizational level appears to require understanding of the shipping system and to improve the methods of managing cross-functional processes and the people working in them. At the process level, Acme needs to reinstate the original work system in terms of understanding, operating, and troubleshooting within the Shipping Department. At the individual level, Acme needs to develop the expertise required of Shipping Department employees to understand, operate, and troubleshoot within the shipping process.

Using the Organizational Diagnosis Model

The five-phase model of performance diagnosis (Figure 5.1) shows the major components of diagnosis as presented throughout this chapter. Figure 5.8 visually captures all the detail for each of the five major phases and records the key points. Use this figure as a complete visual summary of this chapter.

It is important to remember that all of this model's features are not used all the time. Doing so would be inefficient and impractical. The analyst, using the basic five-phase model in one situation, can confidently speed through the process when the questions, data, and synthesis of the data are readily available, clear, reliable, and valid. Thus, for one performance issue the diagnostic model can result in a one-hour investigation. In another, it may take a team of performance diagnosticians a month.

Chapter Four presented and discussed the reality of the boss confronting you with any of the following starting points of a performance diagnosis: (1) We don't have a problem; (2) We think we have a problem. Can you help?; (3) Here is the problem. What is the solution?; and (4) Here is the problem and here is the solution! Each of these starting points plunks the analyst down at a different place in the diagnostic process and requires the analyst to move out accordingly in the model so as to effectively and efficiently reach the performance proposal phase. Knowledge of the complete model (Figure 5.8) helps ensure *effectiveness*. Experience is the avenue to *efficiency*.

Figure 5.8. Overall Process of Diagnosing Performance.

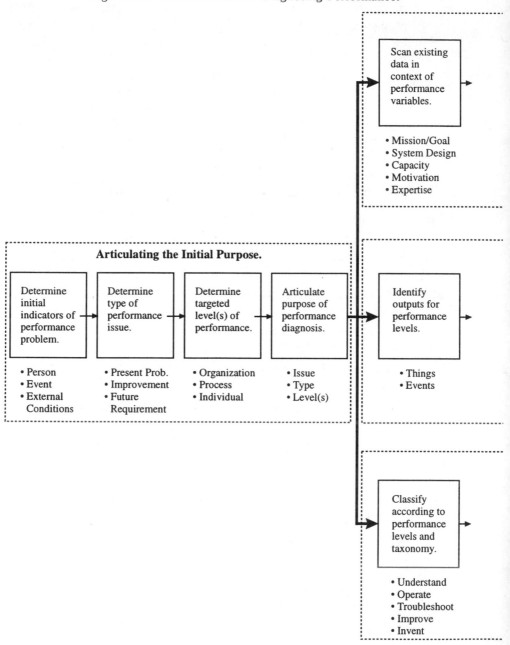

Figure 5.8. Overall Process of Diagnosing Performance, Cont'd.

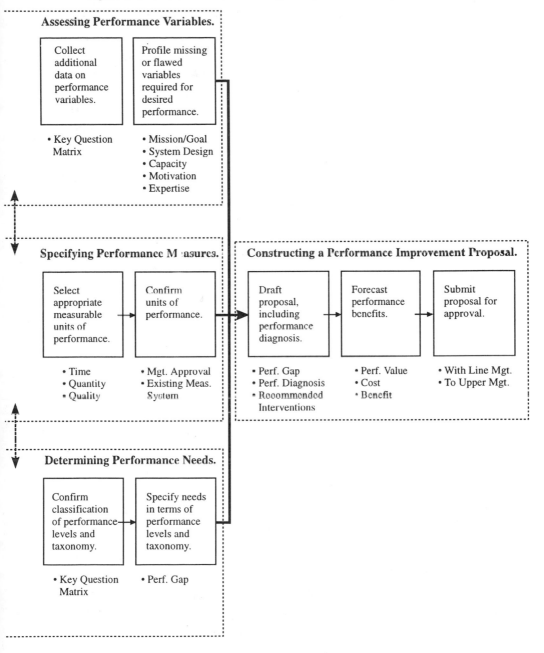

The Health Management, Inc., Case

Health Management, Inc. (HMI), is an organization that manages health care services by bridging the gap between a number of parties, including the health care providers, the companies purchasing group health care coverage, private and government health insurance organizations, and individual patients.

HMI works in a rapidly changing, complex, and competitive industry. The core of its business is information, the analysis of information, and the speedy access to information for decision making with the promise of higher-quality health care at lower costs.

Performance and performance diagnosis are valued at HMI. The following case illustrates, at a general level, a performance analysis by a consultant who is asked to join the HMI team as a major innovation rolls out.

The Consultant's Starting Point

The consultant, with expertise in starting up new systems-oriented training, is called in by two HMI managers. As the conversation unfolds, the consultant is assessing the people in the room as well as HMI, while the managers are assessing him.

HMI has developed a new macromanagement information system (MMIS) that will revolutionize the way it does its work. Every aspect of the business will be monitored and increasingly controlled through MMIS. The software will be completed in six months, and at that time the company will pilot test two of five software subsystems. The pilot test will involve training and the rollout of two MMIS subsystems.

The consultant's job is to develop high-quality, performance-based training and become a member of the rollout "team." The team also includes the manager of R&D, who is responsible for MMIS, and the manager of operations, who is responsible for overall performance improvement in HMI.

From the discussion, it is clear that there has been high-level performance diagnosis at the *strategic level* resulting in justification for developing MMIS. The key players in this step included the CEO, the VP of R&D, and the VP of operations, along with the executive team, which based its decision on a performance diagnosis of the health care industry. The consultant, in preparation for the meeting, read HMI's annual report and the appropriate industry analysis section contained in the *Value Line Investment Survey, Ratings, and Reports,* a stock and industry analysis service. The two sources confirmed each other.

The next performance diagnosis tier—the *tactical level* of delving deeper into the information system and software options—was left to the two VPs and the two key managers referred to previously.

The need for a performance diagnosis at the *implementation level* is the point of the consultant's entry. Systems thinking is critical to understanding the journey to this point and the diagnosis of the MMIS rollout performance issue. Recall the five components of performance diagnosis:

- Articulate the initial purpose
- Assess the performance variables
- Specify the performance measures
- Determine the performance needs
- Construct a performance improvement proposal

Articulate the Initial Purpose

The performance improvement consultant already has a fair amount of information about the initial purpose and other diagnostic questions. For example, external conditions are driving this total effort, which revolves around MMIS, a "thing," and the start-up of MMIS, an "event"; the performance issue is aimed at future MMIS performance requirements for almost all five hundred employees in the organization; MMIS is a major change in the core business process with specific expertise required at different job levels; and the organization has developed an internal four-part performance scorecard that is already in place.

Determine the Performance Needs

Given this highly structured situation, it seemed important to learn more about the system requirements. The Taxonomy of Performance and its five levels helped establish the need for MMIS "understanding" level of expertise among all five hundred employees. In addition, all employees need to know basic "operation" of the MMIS system, and all employees need to know how to "operate" at least one of the five different MMIS program subcomponents. Closer inspection will likely reveal seventeen specific tasks, with three to four tasks within each of the five MMIS components. Yet, about six of the specific tasks are already being used by employees in the existing system.

Another requirement is to deliver training to multiple groups at twenty sites throughout a six-state region. Furthermore, since HMI is growing rapidly, there will be a continuing need for new employee MMIS training and performance support and training.

Assess the Performance Variables

The team approach is a major clue that HMI understands that training alone will not ensure the successful start-up of MMIS. Having the MMIS expert (the operations manager) and the performance improvement consultant work together makes sense. A mock trial of these two based on the key question matrix would peel back some of the roadblocks to performance.

It is also important to collect objective data from a number of sources in context of the five performance variables (mission/goal, system design, capacity, motivation, and expertise) about the present performance and the future performance at various levels in the organization and at various locations. To do this, open-ended, in-person interviews with selected employees should be followed up by a quick, but systematic, employee survey.

Specify the Performance Measures

To a fault, HMI has performance measures. The new MMIS system introduction is a good time to revisit the connectedness of the existing and planned measures at the organizational, process, and individual levels to see if they are pulling in the same direction. Accurate and timely data for the purpose of making sound decisions is the recurring theme. The four-part performance scorecard being touted by the executive management team is very specific and will continue to be used as the performance measure template. Therefore, it should be carefully reviewed.

Construct a Performance Improvement Proposal

The performance proposal begins to take form from the diagnosis. It comes from all three members of the rollout team, not just the consultant. The major portion of the proposal will be training that is enveloped in a management support system at rollout time. The workplace expertise required of the MISS modules and job holders must be analyzed.

The training will necessarily be packaged in stand-alone modules that can be combined as required by job roles and by individual employees. General modules will be prepared with an eye toward media-based self-instruction. Specialized modules will be structured for group classroom training and follow-up, structured, on-the-job training. The specific media and presentation options will be chosen based on the financial forecasts.

The system rollout will be structured to include local managers as partners in its management and training delivery.

Summary Comment

The purpose of this case is to paint a picture of orderliness in the middle of a complex and high-pressure organization. When all is said and done, the rollout of MMIS must work. To do this, five hundred employees need to develop very specific workplace expertise and their managers must create the conditions to ensure improved performance.

Conclusion

It should be easy to see that the information required to conduct a performance diagnosis is not available in a predictable manner. This is the challenge. Some critical information will be waiting for you as you begin your investigation. Other information may not exist at all and should. Some will be held captive by individuals in the organization for either political or proprietary reasons. Thus, to suggest a precise sequence to the process is not realistic. Your job is to obtain the key information in as effective and efficient a manner as possible.

The data collected in the diagnostic process are analyzed as needed to move the process along to the final phase of diagnosing performance—developing the performance improvement proposal. The next two chapters discuss performance improvement proposals and data collection methods, respectively.

Chapter 6

Constructing a Performance Improvement Proposal

Organizational specialists in areas like product research, marketing, and sales maintain their vital contributions to the organization by developing plans of action to improve organizational performance, by gaining approval for their plans, and then by carrying out the plans. Human resource development, quality improvement, reengineering, and performance technology specialists should act no differently. For this reason, an important outcome of a performance diagnosis is a formal *performance improvement proposal.* The proposal provides an overview of the performance gap, an analysis of the performance variables, intervention options and recommendations, and forecasted benefits. The purpose of this chapter is to help you gain organizational approval for your performance improvement intervention.

The performance improvement proposal is the fifth and final phase of the performance diagnosis process (see Figure 5.1). Chapter Five covered the first four phases, which provide the diagnostic information required for the proposal.

Process of Constructing
a Performance Improvement Proposal

The process of constructing a performance improvement proposal contains three steps (see Figure 6.1). These steps help the
analyst organize the information for the purpose of putting
together an effective and brief proposal.

Figure 6.1. Constructing a Performance Improvement Proposal.

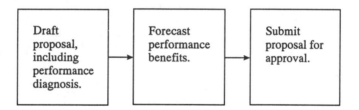

The data sets for each step come directly out of the performance diagnosis process. In this proposal phase, you should
not generate additional information. Furthermore, the proposal
should not display everything you know about the performance
issue. Your job is to choose and present appropriate information for the purpose of helping the organization make a sound
investment decision.

The performance improvement interventions in the proposal should address the organizational, process, and/or individual levels of performance requiring change. Furthermore,
the interventions presented in the proposal should address
the performance variable (mission/goals, systems design, capacity, motivation, and expertise) and the reality that multiple
variables are impacting on each aspect of performance. Your
responses to the questions about performance variables and
performance levels (see Figure 5.4) help in this intervention
decision process. The questions push the diagnostician to the
heart of the performance requirements and toward the appropriate interventions.

Elements of a
Performance Improvement Proposal

At a minimum, a performance improvement proposal should address four major elements:

- Performance gap
- Performance diagnosis
- Recommended interventions
- Forecasted benefits

Performance Gap

The proposal for performance improvement is founded on the premise that the program you are proposing is in response to a carefully determined performance requirement. While most improvement efforts are said to be based on up-front analysis, in practice we find many programs being implemented that are based on superficial, routine analysis activity that barely scratches the surface of the systematic diagnosis of performance described in Chapter Five.

Performance improvement cannot occur in a vacuum. The central objective of accurately determining performance requirements is achieving congruence between the present performance, the performance goal of the organization, and the performance improvement effort. Nonetheless, a majority of today's development programs, whether or not their stated purpose is to "improve performance," are unconnected to the ingredients necessary for achieving organizational success.

Put a measurable performance stake in the ground along with a promise of improvement. This will show the distance from the present performance to the performance after the approval of the proposal and implementation of the intervention.

Performance Diagnosis

A performance issue is carefully specified at the individual, process, and/or organizational level. It can be expressed in the

form of performance goals or as gaps between present and desired performance and should be central to the mission of the
organization. As recommended earlier, framing the diagnosis in
terms of (1) a present problem, (2) improvement, or (3) future
performance is important. Your performance improvement
frame should be communicated in the proposal.

The performance diagnosis (Gilbert, 1978; Mager & Pipe,
1984; Harless, 1980) originally focused attention on the importance of systematically examining the cause(s) of individual performance problems. Employees may fail to meet performance
expectations for a number of reasons: they do not have the *aptitude* (capacity) to perform; they do not have the *know-how* (expertise) to perform; they *choose* (motivation) not to perform; they
do not have the proper *tools, equipment, or environment* (systems design) to perform; or performance *expectations* (goals) are
not clearly defined in the first place. Thus, beyond lack of knowledge or skill (which is most often addressed by training), individual performance problems can be attributed to low aptitude,
a lack of motivation and incentives, and poor work environment.

Campbell (Campbell, Campbell, & Associates, 1988, p. 178)
points out that performance determinants (variables) are not totally independent and that "training competes with and interacts
with better selection and enhanced motivation as strategies for
improving productivity through higher individual performance."
At the process level, efforts at improvement can be classified as
(1) incremental (Harrington, 1992; Juran, 1992), (2) radically revised (Davenport, 1993), or (3) totally reengineered (Hammer &
Champy, 1993). Changing processes impact on and interact with
both the individual and organizational performance levels.

The macro organizational performance level tends to focus on (1) strategic planning (Porter, 1980; Tichy, 1983) or (2)
leadership (Kouzes & Posner, 1987; Wheatley, 1992) as the basis of performance improvement.

To reiterate, the harmony between the three performance
levels—organizational, process, and individual—is critical for successful performance improvement efforts. Each of these per-

formance levels provides a means of describing the performance issues. In terms of effective communication, I have generally found using the five performance variables as the framework for analysis and discussion to be best. This approach allows the analyst to substantively and succinctly profile the performance gap between what is and what should be.

Recommended Interventions

Most performance needs critical for organizational success cannot be adequately addressed by one-dimensional interventions. As explained earlier, performance in the workplace is multifaceted. Thus, proposed performance improvement interventions almost always need to be multidimensional. Each relevant performance variable identified in the performance diagnosis (that is, mission/goal, systems design, capacity, motivation, and expertise) should be considered in choosing performance improvement interventions.

For example, to achieve the performance goals of Acme's Shipping Department, the following five performance variable statements were identified in the performance diagnosis:

Performance Variables — Shipping Department

1. *Mission/goal.* Both the company and the individuals clearly are concerned about surviving and prospering. But there seems to be no understanding of the negative impact that small process decisions are having on the well-being of both the company and the employees.

2. *Systems design.* Over the years, the shipping supervisors arbitrarily altered their job tasks and those of the shippers. In the last several months the Shipping Department has been seriously understaffed, with only one of two shipping supervisors on the job.

3. *Capacity.* Employees are underutilized. Most shippers have the aptitude to understand the shipping system and to complete the shipping tickets.

4. *Motivation.* Adversarial relationships between departments make it hard to admit limitations. Employees
want to do a good job, yet are cautious about being
made scapegoats. Even so, such adversarial conditions
do not exist within the Shipping Department.

5. *Expertise.* Only the hospitalized supervisor has the expertise to complete order tickets.

Note that only one of the performance factors for the Shipping Department — that is, expertise — is addressed exclusively
by training. In nearly all cases, proposals for performance improvements important to the business will include multidimensional interventions. And there will likely be a number of
intervention options to choose from. The selection of appropriate interventions for the required performance improvement
should be made and defended on the following criteria, taken
from Swanson and Gradous (1988, p. 130):

- *Appropriateness* to the organizational culture and
  tradition
- *Availability* of the intervention
- Perceived *quality* of the intervention design
- *Prior effectiveness* of the same or a similar intervention
- *Cost* of the intervention
- Expected *benefit* to the organization

Without the criteria, ineffective and inefficient intervention
options for improving the Shipping Department's performance
could have risen to the surface. For example, an interactive training video for the shippers could gain some supporters of media
and innovation. Yet it would be precluded almost outright by
the appropriateness, availability, and cost criteria. Video training for just a few employees on a task best taught in the work
setting could not meet the criteria.

Forecasted Benefits

The concept of benefits is an extension of performance gains. An effective performance improvement intervention will close the gap between the present level of performance (actual) and the required level of performance (goal).

Any performance can be given a value. Apart from this there are costs for obtaining a level of performance. The benefit is arrived at through the simple process of subtracting the cost from the performance value (Swanson & Gradous, 1988, p. 20). Performance values, costs, and benefits can be discussed in both monetary and nonmonetary terms. An analyst who can talk in monetary terms can also talk in nonmonetary terms, but the opposite is not necessarily true. I recommend a financial forecast for every performance improvement proposal, as I would for any other business investment.

Performance value, cost, and benefit conditions exist before and after an intervention, and thus forecast comparisons can be made between the present state and a desired future state. Additionally, forecasts between intervention options promising to reach the identical or varying performance goals can be made (Figure 6.2).

Sample Performance Improvement Proposal

This section includes a sample performance improvement proposal (Exhibit 6.1). Since this is for the same company that we have been discussing all along—Acme, Inc.—you will not be

Figure 6.2. Benefit Forecast Model.

Present State	Future State
Option A	Option B
Performance Value	Performance Value
−Cost	−Cost
Benefit	Benefit

Exhibit 6.1. Acme, Inc.
Performance Improvement Proposal.

DATE: month/day/year

TO: Director, Distribution Division

FROM: Manager, Performance Improvement
           Head, Shipping Department

RE: Performance Improvement Proposal—Shipping Department

Performance Requirements: Company

The company has been experiencing a number of disturbing and costly performance indicators over the past four months. Included are a 7% increase in returned goods (from 5% to 12%), a 3% increase in inventory error rate (from 3% to 6%), and a 10% increase in shipper overtime (from 5% to 15%). A thorough performance analysis has identified specific performance needs in each of the departments, the division management team, and the company. This proposal is for the Shipping Department and the actions/programs management and training will need to take to improve the performance of the company.

Performance Goal: Shipping Department

The performance goals for the Shipping Department in the next six months are to (1) reduce shipping overtime by 10%, as measured by clock hours of overtime, and (2) reduce the inventory error rate by 3%, as measured by individual order errors in relation to those processed.

Performance Diagnosis: Shipping Department

1. *Mission/goal.* Both the company and individuals clearly are concerned about surviving and prospering. While these common goals need to be harmonized, the individual "survival goals" seem to be predominant at this time and negatively affecting the company. This performance concern is being addressed by the Total Quality Management Proposal that has recently been endorsed by the president.

2. *Systems design:* The department is seriously understaffed, with only one of two shipping supervisors being on the job. The second supervisor has been out for five months with a major illness and will not be returning to work. In addition, informally and over time, job roles and duties in the department have become redefined, reduced, and isolated.

3. *Capacity:* Employees are underutilized. Most shippers have the aptitude to understand the shipping system and how to complete the shipping tickets.

Exhibit 6.1. Acme, Inc.
Performance Improvement Proposal, Cont'd.

---

4. *Motivation:* Adversarial relationships between departments make it hard to admit limitations. Employees want to do a good job, yet are cautious about being made scapegoats.

5. *Expertise:* Only the hospitalized supervisor has the expertise to complete order tickets. The shippers do not have a systems perspective of the company or their department. The legitimate seat cover substitution task occurs infrequently, is complex, and requires orderly problem-solving skills.

Intervention Options: Shipping Department

   — *Management Elements* —
1. Replace shipping supervisor.
2. Specify job roles and responsibilities of shipping personnel (four categories).

   — *Development Elements* —
3. Train two shipping supervisors on tasks of communication, delegation, and coaching.
4. Train all twenty-four shipping personnel to understand the shipping system.
5. Train twenty shippers to complete seat cover order tickets.
6. Train shipping department head and two shipping supervisors on a team problem-solving method for making seat cover substitutions.

Recommended Performance Improvement Intervention

   — *Program Description* —
It is recommended that all six of the options listed above be implemented. Replacing the supervisor (element #1) requires managerial action and is not an added cost. The same is true of specifying the shipping jobs (element #2). All training will be structured training. Corporate will be responsible for the supervisor training (element #3). The Acme training coordinator will facilitate the development and delivery of the shipping system, order ticket, and substitution problem-solving training programs. All the shipper training will take place on overtime (elements #4 to #6).

   — *Program Management* —
1. Replace shipping supervisor: division director and shipping head hire supervisor in next thirty days.

2. Specify job roles and responsibilities of shipping personnel: shipping head and shipping supervisor write and approve specifications in next fourteen days.

3. Train two shipping supervisors on tasks of communication, delegation, and coaching: Training coordinator negotiates with corporate HRD for their services to meet this need. Supervisor training will take place at corporate. The

Exhibit 6.1. Acme, Inc.
Performance Improvement Proposal, Cont'd.

---

new supervisor will work on the job for one week, attend the training at corporate, return and work with the present supervisor for one week, and then the present supervisor will attend corporate training. Travel and expense costs will be incurred.

4. Train all twenty-four shipping personnel to understand the shipping system: training coordinator does the development of a one- to two-hour training program to be delivered by department head and trainer.

5. Train twenty shippers to complete seat cover order tickets: training coordinator does the development of a two- to four-hour training program to be delivered by supervisors and trainer.

6. Train Shipping Department head and three shipping supervisors on a team problem-solving method (for solving operational problems, such as seat cover substitutions): training coordinator does the development of a two-hour training program to be delivered by supervisors and trainer.

    —*Program Evaluation*—
Confirm the completion of elements #1 and #2; determine trainee satisfaction and learning resulting from each training program, #3 to #6; and conduct a twelve-month follow-up on overtime and inventory error.

Financial Analysis (detailed breakdown available)

Performance Value (resulting from program in twelve months)	$28,500
—Cost (of program)	−7,750
Benefit (from program in twelve months)	$20,750

---

surprised by the contents of the proposal. You may be surprised by what has been left out, however.

Proposals should be brief and to the point. Of course, backup documentation should be readily available that is organized and that elaborates on or supports key points. A cover letter to the proposal may tell a bit more about that backup information and the key people and processes used to get to the proposal.

Obviously, there are many ways of packaging and presenting proposals. Be purposeful about your approach.

Conclusion

There are two ways to communicate the results of a performance diagnosis to the decision makers: through face-to-face presentations and written performance improvement proposals. Both are generally required to gain organizational commitment. The presentation may be most powerful in gaining approval while the proposal is the contract. The written proposal is the lasting agreement and documentation of the diagnosis phase of performance improvement.

Chapter 7

Data Collection
Methods

Performance improvement analysts are required to collect and analyze data in order to diagnose organizations and document workplace expertise. Several general data collection methods are used throughout the analysis process. They include:

- Interviews

- Questionnaires

- Observations

- Organizational records

This chapter provides an overview of these four data collection methods. My intention is to provide enough guidance to ensure sound data collection practices and to provide recommended sources for more technical assistance.

Analysts committed to improving performance require first-hand information about organizations, processes, and job performers. They must delve into the organization and its workplace issues to obtain accurate information. The task of searching and analyzing information on organization-specific performance issues is demanding, but it can be as much fun as reading a good mystery. In diagnosing and documenting workplace performance and expertise, the four general data collection methods are regularly called on. Each method has appropriate uses, and each demands competence in searching for valid information.

Interviews

The interview method enables analysts to gather information directly from people in the workplace or people connected in various ways to the organization and its processes: in person, in groups, and also by telephone. Interviewing demands a high level of competence and commitment from the analyst. See Exhibit 7.1 for a concise summary of the technique of interviewing.

Interviewing people in the workplace is a time-consuming but useful technique for discovering what happens at the organizational, process, and/or individual job levels. The skillful interviewer anticipates the need to establish rapport with the interviewee — not an easy task when questions of adequacy or efficiency of performance are involved. The interviewer is obliged to record accurate notes, to ask questions of people using their language, and to listen with respect.

Interviewing is done with a critical eye to the process. The following checklist of questions will assist you in keeping your interviewing on track:

> —Have I done my homework?
> —Am I talking to the best possible person, or would someone else be able to offer a more accurate account of the situation?
> —Am I getting straight information?
> —How do the responses of several people compare?
> —Is something being implied but left unspoken?
> —Am I perceived to be a confidant of management, or am I being trusted with knowledge of this situation?
> —Am I managing this limited interview time well?
> —What is the main message this person is giving me?

Exhibit 7.1. Interview Technique Summary.

1. *Description*
   The interviewer and interviewee(s) talk (alone or in small groups) and the interviewer asks questions to get information.

2. *Types*
   A. *Structured:*   The interviewer has a predetermined list of questions arranged in some format. All interviewees are asked the same basic questions plus follow-up questions. This limits the content to some predetermined topics.
   B. *Unstructured:* The interviewer and client talk without any preset format. The interview may cover a wide range of subjects. Different people may be asked entirely different questions.
   C. *Combination:*   Combining structured and unstructured is the most common method.

3. *Uses*
   A. To establish rapport for other data gathering
   B. To get details of work protocol
   C. To learn about plans and projects
   D. To get workers' viewpoints about procedures and processes
   E. To find out about difficulties
   F. To get opinions about organization, morale, supervision
   G. To follow up on critical incidents

4. *Key Skills*
   A. The ability to develop questions that will get meaningful answers
   B. The ability to ask open-ended questions spontaneously
   C. The ability to create an atmosphere of trust — *not* defensiveness
   D. The ability to take complete and accurate notes without infusing one's own ideas

5. *Pros and Cons*

Pros	*Cons*
A. Allows study of a wide range of subjects	A. Can be expensive and time consuming
B. Source of valuable and meaningful information	B. Interviewer can create bias — that is, interject own feelings into the response
C. Allows interviewer to gain "empathy" or a feel for the situation	C. Can be hard to interpret the meaning of answers
D. Process can allow the interviewer to gain the trust of clients	D. Depends on skillful use of questions; takes practice
	E. Difficult to synthesize

—Is it important?

—Have I discovered feelings and motivations as well as facts about this work situation?

—Have I recorded many of the actual words of the respondent?

—What is missing from the picture being painted here?

—How does this interview data compare with data collected by questionnaire, by observation in the work setting, or by organizational performance records?

Interviews yield great quantities of information, which can be difficult to manage and analyze. Plan to spend twice as long writing about the interview as you did conducting it.

Telephone Interviews

Telephone interviews require several unique steps. According to Lavarakas (1987, pp. 18–19), they involve a ten-step process:

1. Deciding upon a sampling design, including the method of respondent selection with a sampling unit
2. Developing and formatting a draft questionnaire
3. Choosing a method to generate the pool of telephone numbers that will be used in sampling
4. Producing a call-sheet for each number that will be used in sampling
5. Developing a draft introduction/selection sheet and fallback statements for use by interviewers
6. Hiring interviewers and supervisors, and scheduling interviewing sessions
7. Pilot-testing and revising survey instruments
8. Printing final questionnaires and other forms
9. Training interviewers and supervisors
10. Conducting fully supervised interviews

Group Interviews

Focus groups are a popular form of group interview where a targeted group of stakeholders come together to provide information about a specific topic. The following focus-group moderating skills outlined by Krueger (1988) capture the uniqueness of this group process technique: (1) selecting the focus-group location, (2) preparing mentally, (3) engaging in purposeful small talk and revealing the presentation strategy, (4) recording the group discussion, (5) pausing and probing, and (6) being ready for the unexpected. The rich interaction from focus groups is particularly helpful in sorting out future performance issues (versus performance problems or performance improvements).

Questionnaires

Deceptively simple, the survey questionnaire is often used as a prime data collection tool. After all, what could be easier than writing up a questionnaire and mailing it off to a hundred people or more? Wrong! Good questionnaires are difficult to develop, and getting sufficient numbers of responses from the target population is even more difficult. But done correctly, no tool is more efficient for getting data from a large, dispersed population. See Exhibit 7.2 for a concise summary of the questionnaire method.

Expert analysts use interviews as a first step for discovering the most useful content for a questionnaire. The questionnaire then offers a way to accurately evaluate the extent and the credibility of the facts and opinions gathered by interviews.

By keeping questionnaires short, you will ensure the goodwill of the respondents and will simplify the data analysis. Pilot testing a questionnaire with a few respondents and, if necessary, rewriting questions can save you from gathering a mountain of useless data.

Unless you are trained in statistical analysis, you would do well to acquire expert guidance in handling all phases of the questionnaire process. Too often the result of an inept questionnaire is garbled information that is useless to the analyst and ultimately to all the people who have spent their time and energy filling out your instrument.

The questionnaire process must begin with the following questions: "What do I want to know?" and "If I get it, how will

Exhibit 7.2. Questionnaire Technique Summary.

1. *Description*
   The investigator has a specific set of written items that require the client to respond in some meaningful way.
2. *Types*
   A. *Open Response:* The items are open-ended questions. The client writes essay-type answers, which are then interpreted by the investigator. The investigator must somehow code the responses and subject them to a data analysis.
   B. *Forced Response:* The questionnaire items require some specific type of response such as: yes or no, true or false, a checkmark placed in a box or on a scale, or a word written in a space. The investigator codes the responses according to a system and then subjects them to data analysis.
3. *Uses*
   A. To cover large populations of people
   B. To overcome problems of geographical distance
   C. To measure attitudes or opinions
   D. To ask about what people value or do
   E. To gather descriptive data
4. *Key Skills*
   A. The ability to specify exactly what type of information is required
   B. The ability to develop items that will get appropriate responses
   C. The ability to do data analysis
   D. The ability to lay out the questionnaire in a clear, readable way
5. *Pros and Cons*

Pros	*Cons*
A. It's relatively easy to quantify and summarize the data gathered.	A. It's a relatively "cold" approach—that is, no personal contact.
B. Questionnaires are easy to use with large samples.	B. It may miss important issues because the questions are predetermined.
C. They are relatively inexpensive.	C. It's difficult to write good items.
D. You can obtain large amounts of data.	D. People may misread items and make inappropriate responses.
E. This method is less time consuming than some other methods.	E. The data may be overinterpreted.
F. Statistical analysis is quick and easy with computers.	F. The response rate may be too low.
G. Questionnaires can often be used in more than one setting.	
H. They are more objective than interviews.	

I use this information?" The process ends with: "Did I discover what I wanted to know?" and "How can I use this information?" The same questions are asked for every item on the questionnaire.

Assuming you have not let all this talk of statistical analysis discourage you from sending out a simple questionnaire, ask yourself the following: "Did I receive a sufficient number of returned questionnaires?" "What did I find out?" "Are these data useful?" "Did I discover something that I should verify through a review of performance records or through observations or interviews?" "Do these data confirm or contradict what I have learned through other means?"

Organizational Culture Questionnaires

Culture surveys are an important tool for performance improvements (versus performance problems or future performances). They provide an effective and efficient method of gathering information from employees (Sleezer & Swanson, 1992).

Surveys must be organized around clear purposes and managed in a simple and effective manner (while maintaining the reliability and validity of the data). Employee perceptions are a window into the health of the organization! A comprehensive survey covers thirteen culture categories, including the following: organizational mission and goals, corporate management's leadership, department management leadership, supervisory effectiveness, working conditions, productivity and accountability, communication, interpersonal and interdepartmental relationships, job satisfaction, employee compensation, employee career development, training and development, and training options (McLean, 1988). The critical features are ensuring anonymity, having an objective third party present, and providing constructive feedback to the organization. Customized surveys to address specific strategic change efforts can be developed from selected culture categories. Baseline data can be used to compare results to later surveys. Open-ended responses can also be solicited and analyzed. The following is a sample "strongly agree to strongly disagree" culture survey question: "When problems occur in my job, I have the freedom to solve them."

Customer Satisfaction Questionnaires

From a performance improvement perspective, what your customers think is critical! Beyond talking to every customer, customer surveys are the most direct and valid means of measuring what customers are thinking (Hayes, 1992). The input of customer requirements can shape organizational goals/processes. Customer satisfaction is a critical "scorecard" of organizational achievement.

High-quality customer surveys can be used to determine customer requirements and customer satisfaction. They can be used for both external customers and internal customers. Customer surveys can answer the core questions: What do customers want? Are customers satisfied with what they receive?

Carefully designed paper-and-pencil surveys tied concisely and directly to customer requirements are the most cost-effective means of surveying customers. Surveying smaller samples, instead of entire groups, increases efficiency and minimizes customer annoyance. Subtle or ill-defined customer requirements may require face-to-face techniques, such as focus groups or critical incident techniques (Flanagan, 1954). Critical incidents are reports or descriptions of things people have done or have observed others doing. Thus, the critical incident technique can be called on for any of the four general data collection methods. Regardless of the specific data collection technique used, customer satisfaction surveys should match the important customer requirements accepted by the organization.

Observations

Thinking, planning, imagining, and estimating are abstract work behaviors and, one would think, unaccountable. People express the results of their work performances through observable actions, however, and the qualities of their actions can be observed. When practiced systematically, observing people at work will yield a great deal of qualitative and quantitative information about the work, the worker, and the work environment. See Exhibit 7.3 for a concise summary of the technique of observing.

Exhibit 7.3. Observation Technique Summary.

1. *Description*
   The observer goes on-site and watches the work behavior of people doing the job.

2. *Types*
   A. *Overt:*   The observer tells the worker what is going on. The worker knows what the observer is looking for. The observer may even ask the worker to do certain things in order to help with the observation. This type of observation is frequently combined with an interview during which the observer asks the worker to explain things as they are done.
   B. *Covert:* The observer doesn't tell the worker what is going on. Normally the observer is in plain view but the worker is unaware of what actually is being observed. The observer normally doesn't communicate with the worker or interfere in any way with the work. This helps to let the observer watch the natural work method in its actual sequence, without special effort.

3. *Uses*
   A. To analyze work methods for effectiveness and efficiency
   B. To corroborate employee performance with interview reports
   C. To analyze conditions in the work environment
   D. To find safety/housekeeping problems
   E. To analyze communication patterns
   F. To watch work flow
   G. To locate critical incidents

4. *Key Skills*
   A. The ability to find the best people and times to observe
   B. The ability to keep out of the worker's way
   C. The ability to be open to new ways of doing the work
   D. The ability to spot when the work is being done correctly and incorrectly
   E. The ability to take accurate notes or remember the important things seen

5. *Pros and Cons*

Pros	*Cons*
A. The observer can collect firsthand information on behavior.	A. It can be difficult to interpret what is observed, especially when the worker is solving a problem by thinking it through.
B. Observations occur while the work is actually being done—not after it's over.	B. Sampling the people and times can bias the results. (It could be a unique situation.)
C. Observations can be adapted to many situations.	C. The observer can create bias by interjecting own feelings.
D. They may reveal totally unexpected problems.	D. Follow-up is usually required to help interpret the observations.
E. They may reveal new and better methods.	E. It can be costly.
F. They are not filtered through another's words.	

Observing people at work requires considerable skill. Great sensitivity and the ability to be unobtrusive are essential. To avoid altering the work process, you must become part of the flow. The unobtrusive observer is more likely to perceive errors, problems, and creative solutions than is the intrusive observer.

Some activities happen more or less frequently than others, some take a longer or shorter time to complete, and some happen only at the beginning or the end of the month. Therefore, judging the length of the required observation time can be difficult. One thing is certain: the longer you observe in a setting, the more you see. Before beginning to analyze work behaviors, take care to observe long enough to be able to discriminate between those behaviors that:

- Add something of value to the product or services or process (productivity)

- Add nothing (waste of a worker's effort or time)

- Are linked and ordered in meaningful ways

- Take away from the value of the product or service or process (mistakes, negative remarks, interfering with others at work, and so forth)

Your major assets as an observer are wide-open eyes and ears, a curious and nonjudgmental nature, and the ability to discriminate between behaviors.

If you can't figure out what a particular work behavior is, ask. If the technology of the work is unfamiliar, if the nature of the work behaviors are subtle, or if you encounter a controversy about how the work should be done, you will benefit by researching the work and the setting before continuing to observe.

By accurately recording events, you can test the beliefs of management and workers and even your own first impressions of the work performance. Is the behavioral protocol the same for all employees? How frequently do the observed behaviors occur? What qualities of the behavior are important? Speed? Accuracy? Decision making? Language? Do obstacles to performance exist in the work environment? What are the expected versus the actual results of the work behavior? Is the work performance rewarded, punished, or ignored? What behaviors differentiate the high performers from the low performers?

Be cautious when interpreting the data derived from observation. Consider that your presence can change the situation and affect the data collected. Were you sufficiently prepared for the observation to understand what you were observing? How accurate are your data? Were you unable to record what you saw because of a lack of time or recording skill? Is that important? Does the observed behavior fall into phases or stages? Is it cyclical?

The canard that "a picture is worth a thousand words" applies equally to analysis work. The picture in the realm of performance improvement analysis consists of the actual organization, the functioning processes, and the individuals working in them. Firsthand observation provides a tier of information that cannot be obtained through talk and paper—interviews, questionnaires, and organizational records.

Organizational Records

Organizations keep records of many everyday occurrences. These include employee turnover; absenteeism; grievances filed; units of performance per person, per hour, per day, per week; and costs of production. Policy manuals, procedure manuals, interoffice memos, minutes of board meetings, and the like are kept on file. Trends and cycles can often be spotted in these records. You may find clues to trouble spots that will provide useful questions for your interviews. Ordinary, everyday business records are a great source of information for the alert analyst with skills in interpreting data. For more information on the organizational records technique, see Exhibit 7.4.

Organizational records generally reflect the consequences of a problem situation, just as they may later reflect its resolution. Thus, these records are most useful in zeroing in on present

Exhibit 7.4. Organizational Records Technique Summary.

1. *Description*
   The analyst classifies, studies, and interprets the meaning of the numbers or information buried in the records.

2. *Types*
   A. *Primary:* The analyst gathers and studies cost, time, and productivity data or reports as a primary source of information. Information is usually classified and depicted in a way that reveals specific points of interest. This type of data analysis is normally used to locate areas of loss or trends.
   B. *Secondary:* The analyst classifies and studies data gained through interviews, observations, or questionnaires in order to design an overall picture from many separate pieces of information. This type of analysis is frequently used to consolidate information gathered from all the other methods of investigation.

3. *Uses*
   A. To analyze areas of loss
   B. To corroborate and expand work-behavior protocol
   C. To spot and predict trends
   D. To consolidate information gathered from other investigative methods
   E. To spot cyclical problems
   F. To classify information into categories

4. *Key Skills*
   Note: Data analysis can require a wide variety of technical skills; this list covers a few of the basics.
   A. The ability to classify or group information into categories
   B. The ability to find relationships between categories or separate pieces of information
   C. The ability to select and use statistical and other math techniques
   D. The ability to depict data with charts and graphs
   E. The ability to interpret data and make verbal explanations of their meaning

5. *Pros and Cons*

Pros	Cons
A. The organizational records technique minimizes people's biases.	A. It can be difficult to locate the best data or reports.
B. Numbers tend to be believable and easy to understand.	B. The data could have been biased by those who recorded them in the first place.
C. This technique can identify accurate "baselines" against which to measure changes in performance.	C. It can be difficult to quantify some important aspects of performance.

performance problems (versus performance improvements or future performances). Caution must be taken in interpreting these data, because they are generally collected for other purposes. How old are the data? How reliable were the collecting and recording methods? Be alert for aggregated information that may hide major organizational problems among innocent-looking, averaged figures. A knowledge of statistical methods is useful to the careful analyst.

Once you have verified the accuracy and considered the context of the organizational records, spotted trends, and identified problems, ask yourself if any of the data seem surprising, contradictory, optimistic, pessimistic, or problematic. The data should confirm or deny the facts gained through other data collection methods.

Benchmarking is the search for the best practices that will lead to the superior performance of an organization (Camp, 1989). It is a process that integrates data obtained from all four of the general data collection methods (interviews, questionnaires, observations, and organizational records). According to Camp, the ten process steps include:

1. Identify what is to be benchmarked.

2. Identify comparative companies.

3. Determine the data collection method and collect the data.

4. Determine the current performance gap.

5. Project future performance levels.

6. Communicate the benchmark findings and gain acceptance for them.

7. Establish functional goals.

8. Develop action plans.

9. Implement specific actions and monitor progress.

10. Recalibrate the benchmarks.

Checkpoint

Use the following multiple-choice items to check your understanding of the techniques for data collection. Select the best answer for each item. The answers to these questions are at the end of the test.

___1. The observer does not communicate with the person being observed when_____.
   a. the worker does not want to be observed
   b. the observer could get in the way
   c. observing the most natural work process is desired
   d. management objects to the observation process

___2. Observations are used to_____.
   a. gather data from large populations
   b. learn about plans and goals
   c. find work environment problems
   d. spot cyclical problems

___3. The analyst has observed four workers in the department, but the manager is unimpressed with the findings because _____.
   a. the observer failed to ask the workers about their work
   b. the observer failed to separate high and low performers
   c. the observer is wrong about the count of behaviors
   d. the observer failed to observe a sufficient sample of workers

___4. The analyst should avoid using the interview techniques to collect data if_____.
   a. getting a feel for the situation is important
   b. time and money are in short supply
   c. treating open-ended questions is a skill the analyst has not developed
   d. learning about complaints is the issue

___5. The skill that is most essential in interviewing is_____.
   a. fostering trust

   b. asking questions that get meaningful answers
   c. taking complete notes
   d. asking open-ended questions
__6. Because of the difficulty of designing good questions, a
    thoughtful analyst would_____before sending out 100
    questionnaires.
    a. carefully select the people who will receive the ques-
       tionnaire
    b. establish the budget for design, printing, mailing, and
       data analysis
    c. plan to mail the questionnaire in two batches
    d. pilot test it with a few respondents
__7. The exclusive use of limited-response questions may result
    in a questionnaire that is easy to tabulate but that fails to
    identify an important issue. To avoid this possibility, the
    analyst could_____.
    a. include at least one or two open-ended questions
    b. invite respondents to write comments anywhere on the
       questionnaire as thoughts occur to them
    c. pilot test the questionnaire and interview respondents
    d. all of the above
__8. An analyst without the requisite statistical analysis skills is
    at a disadvantage because_____.
    a. an outside expert must be consulted
    b. the importance of some record could be missed
    c. only certain records can be made visual by graphing
    d. interpreting and explaining data are essential
__9. Establishing the accuracy of primary records is_____.
    a. difficult
    b. impossible
    c. essential
    d. assumed by the organization

Answers

1.c   2.c   3.b   4.b   5.a   6.a   7.a   8.d   9.c

Conclusion

The general data collection methods—interviews, question-naires, observations, and organizational records—provide an eclectic toolbox for the analyst. They are used at both the organizational diagnosis and documentation of expertise levels.

Each method has strengths and weaknesses. In almost all instances, using more than one data collection method is necessary to ensure valid conclusions about the trends, factors, and causes of organizational, process, and individual performances or the dimensions and substance of workplace expertise.

PART THREE

DOCUMENTING
WORKPLACE
EXPERTISE

Chapter 8

The Nature
of Workplace
Expertise

Workplace expertise is the fuel of an organization. Expertise is defined as the level at which a person is able to perform within a specialized realm of human activity. Most of us are accustomed to high levels of expertise. Through technological devices, we can listen to and view performances by experts in many fields of endeavor. We are surrounded by art, music, lectures, books, movies, and sports created by experts or in which experts participate.

On television, we can see expert home restorers whiz through complicated procedures using tools that we have never seen before, let alone ever mastered. Our church choir may have warmth and charm, but can it stand up to the Mormon Tabernacle Choir being played on a high-tech digital sound system? The examples are endless.

It is no wonder that neophytes want to take shortcuts to expertise — or worse yet, to pretend they are experts. What else could explain the desire of young adults to wear sports clothing instead of playing the sport? Or the desire of adults in the workplace to pick up the language of the latest pop management book instead of learning industrial psychology or system theory? Today we have CEOs who are unable to flowchart a simple

process like making a cup of instant coffee, yet they are setting
loose the wrath of reengineering in their companies in response
to popular journal articles. In comparison, overweight teenagers
wearing professional sports jackets walking the halls of your local
shopping mall look pretty tame.

Dilemmas in Developing Expertise

Developing expertise is not an event. It is a purposeful journey. As a result, organizations face a number of dilemmas in
their efforts to deal with workplace expertise. They are:

- Emphasizing general knowledge versus specific expertise
- Hiring versus developing expertise
- Nature versus nurture paths to expertise

Emphasizing General Versus Specific Expertise

Experts are good problem solvers in their domain of expertise.
Good problem solvers utilize specific methods. The more general
the methods used, the less expertise is involved. There are good
reasons for people to study situations at a general level. Many
people who study jobs and work have a goal of defining occu-
pations and jobs at the most general level. It can be useful to
describe in a general way what an executive does, versus a manager, versus a first-line supervisor. This level of analysis assures
you that you are "in the ballpark." All of us have figuratively
found ourselves "out of the ballpark" and know how humiliat-
ing that is. This level of analysis offers protection against being
wrong—but it is not the makings of expertise.

The tools for documenting expertise presented in this book
were used by a Fortune 50 corporation to determine the expertise required of first-line supervisors in its manufacturing plants.
By determining and documenting precisely what plant supervisors were required to know and be able to do in order to function as experts, the supporting work system and training realized
a 9:1 return on investment (900 percent) in two years. This was

no academic or off-the-shelf view of good supervision — it was production specific and company specific. In contrast, I had the chance to audit the results of an expensive off-the-shelf "managing people" program that had been provided to every manager in a Fortune 10 financial corporation for a ten-year period. Search as I did, I could find no evidence that the program had any impact on the corporation. The "managing people" generalities covered in the program were interesting but did not represent what people were required to know and be able to do in order to perform on the job. In other words, the work generalities did not capture workplace expertise.

Hiring Versus Developing Expertise

Many organizations are not well equipped to manage the development and maintenance of expertise in their workforce. Working under the assumption that expertise is the fuel of an organization, one reaction is to outsource expertise rather than develop it. "Hire versus develop" is a fundamental business decision that is aggravated by changing markets and changing technology.

Some firms decide to outsource work requiring specific expertise as they compare the costs and benefits of maintaining internal expertise. Even so, much workplace expertise is company specific, and it is impossible to hire such expertise in the open market. Imagine, too, having expertise critical to the health of an organization undocumented in any formal manner. Organizations wanting to survive and grow must purposefully deal with the problems of procuring, developing, and maintaining workplace expertise.

Nature Versus Nurture: Paths to Expertise

I remember a poster from the late 1960s showing a baby being held upside down by the doctor seconds after being born. The mother was on the delivery table. The caption read: "Your son, the plumber." It was left to the individuals viewing the poster to interpret the meaning of the doctor's pronouncement: genetics? socioeconomic status? both? The concept that a person's life expertise and life role are bounded by genetics is extremely uncomfortable in a culture that generally believes that the presence or absence of opportunities, not innate capacities, limits expertise. Thus, our institutions have had to develop oblique methods of screening employees to make sure they have the required innate capacity. Organizations that overestimate the innate capacity of workers can pay a heavy price. In extreme cases, companies have been forced to close down large-scale operations when their workforce has neither the expertise nor capacity that meets the demands of new processes. Conversely, underestimating the capacity of the workforce results in similar dismal performance results.

Getting to Expertise

Now we're ready to discuss the tools used to document workplace expertise. These include the job description, task inventory, and task analyses. A *job description* defines the boundaries of a job, while a *task inventory* highlights the discernible parts (tasks) of a job and *task analyses* detail the expertise required to perform each task. A job can be described in terms of an artist's canvas. Job description is a broad-brush activity. The analyst-painter uses a finer brush and finer movements to define the expertise embodied in each task. At the most meticulous level, the details of the job emerge with an almost photographic quality. To put it in more concrete terms, the job description is painted with a four-inch-wide brush, the task inventory with a two-inch-wide brush, and the task analyses are painted with a one-sixteenth-inch-wide brush.

Consider the following job title as an example: Corporate Director of Human Resources. Most of us would agree that this is an impressive title, but what does a director of human resources really do? Let's take a look at the job behind this title in one company and compare it to the job behind the same title in a second company.

Company A. The director heads the corporatewide human resource department, supervises fifteen professionals, and manages a $2 million budget.

Company B. The director heads the corporatewide human resource department, supervises an administrative assistant, and is responsible for proposing and implementing performance improvement programs under a zero-based budgeting system.

In two quick sentences, these seemingly similar jobs are shown to be very different. Even so, there is hardly a clue as to exactly what a person is required to know and be able to do to perform in either job. These large-brush job descriptions need to be supplemented by a finer level of detail—detail provided by a task inventory and task analyses. The task inventory will provide a list of the specific tasks the director's job entails; the three methods of analyzing tasks—procedural, systems, and knowledge—will accommodate the varying nature of the expertise expected of the director.

These workplace expertise documentation phases just discussed are displayed as a process in Figure 8.1. In Figure 8.2 a number of work factors, such as work behaviors and work interaction, are laid up against the five phases of analyzing workplace expertise. This matrix provides a comparison of the key features of the analysis of expertise presented in Chapters Nine through Thirteen. Documentation forms (see the Appendix) are used for each tool and underscore the important fact that *each* task from the task inventory is analyzed and documented with one or more of the three task analysis methods.

The final workplace expertise documents, and many of the in-process documents, should be loaded into the computer. These are documents that need to be revised and manipulated. Among other things, they can be used as a basis for quality improvement efforts, training materials, and various forms of certification. In order for the documentation of expertise to be fully

Figure 8.1. Documenting Expertise.

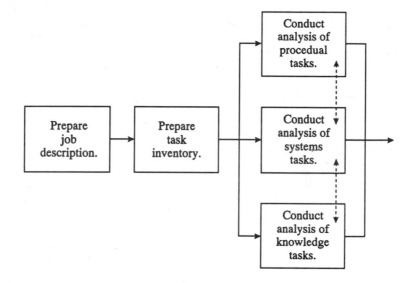

utilized, it should be computer based and readily available to as many people in the organization as possible.

Here are a couple of helpful tips: Many organizations have formatted the various documentation forms into their computer systems to serve the analysts as they start their work, not after the fact. Also, many companies establish updating and revision systems on top of their original documentation process so as to capture improvements and changes as they occur.

Conclusion

This chapter has provided a brief introduction to the documentation of expertise in the workplace. Again, it is worth highlighting the fundamental premise that rigorous documentation of this expertise is the true source of training content and the starting point for many performance improvement efforts.

The next five chapters consider each of the tools used to document workplace expertise: job description, task inventory, and—most significant in terms of usefulness and stability—procedural, systems, and knowledge task analyses.

Figure 8.2. Features of the Five Analysis of Expertise Tools.

Work Factors	Analysis Tools				
	Job Description	Task Inventory	Procedural Task Analysis	Systems Task Analysis	Knowledge Task Analysis
Work behaviors	• Clusters of activity	• Discrete activities	• Observable	• Partially observable	• Nonobservable
Work interactions	• Degree of variety	• Degree of variety	• Worker-materials • Worker-machine	• Worker-process	• Worker-worker • Worker-idea
Work structure	• Degree of structure	• Degree of structure	• Bound to a particular work procedure	• Bound to a particular process	• Many performance situations
Worker autonomy	• Worker relationships	• Task relationships	• Follows procedures	• Works within established systems	• Works within vague or fluid systems
Performance objectives	• Organization and process levels	• Process and individual levels	• Individual and process levels • Ability to follow correct procedures, leading to standard performance	• Individual and process levels • Ability to use efficient methods, leading to standard performance or results	• Individual process and/or organization levels • Ability to use structured knowledge, information, leading to standard performance or results
In-process products	• Existing job description • Interview notes	• Existing task inventory • Interview notes	• Task details • Sketches	• Systems description and flowchart • Systems parts and purpose list • Process analysis chart	• Behavioral data collection instrument • Collected data • Research cards from literature search • Synthesis model(s)
End product of the analysis	• 25–75 word narrative overview	• List of discrete job tasks	• Step-by-step procedure • Diagram of machine or material	• Troubleshooting analysis • In-process documents • Diagrams	• Subject matter description (may include synthesis model) • Reference list

Chapter 9

Documenting
Job Descriptions

A job description is a statement that establishes the scope of responsibilities in a specific job in a specific organization. Determining the scope of job responsibility is the basic purpose of writing a job description. But other reasons for writing job descriptions exist as well. Some organizations purposely mandate vague and/or open-ended job descriptions to preserve organizational flexibility in terms of job restructuring while maintaining legal compliance. These descriptions usually contain more information on prerequisites than job responsibilities. For this reason, they have limited value in actually establishing precisely what a person is required to know and be able to do to perform a specific job (expertise). In contrast, job descriptions written for the purpose of performance improvement are specific and well defined. They are focused on the scope of what the job holder actually does, not the prerequisites to performing the work.

Documenting Job Descriptions

The process of documenting job descriptions requires some reflection on the available and true sources of expertise (Figure 9.1).

Figure 9.1. Developing a Job Description.

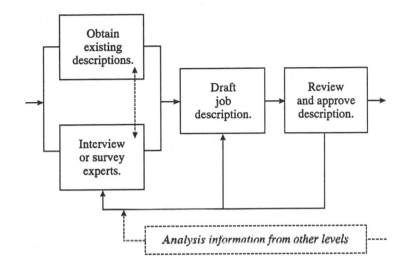

The starting point is the criteria for job descriptions. This is followed by two data gathering steps that can occur simultaneously or sequentially, depending on the specific circumstances.

One of these steps is to obtain existing job descriptions within the firm or from external sources, such as professional references or other companies. The second step is to interview experts—people who have a deep understanding of the job. Usually this includes job incumbents, managers/supervisors of job incumbents, and co-workers. These interviews are usually fairly brief and generally result in discrepancies that ultimately get resolved at a later time.

The next step in the process—drafting the job description—concretizes the description. Rarely will a draft escape criticism and revision at the review step that follows. While the expert job incumbent and that person's manager/supervisor should be involved in the review, the manager is the one to approve the final job description. This approval can always be subject to later review, revision, and approval. In fact, the job description, as with the other levels of analysis, *should* be re-

vised when additional information coming from the more detailed analysis levels challenges its accuracy or completeness.

The following is an acceptable job description. Read it carefully and note the level of detail used. After this, we will look
at the criteria for good job descriptions and task inventories and
at the methods for producing them:

Job Description

Job or Program:	Vinyl Laminator
Location:	Custom Kitchens, Inc.
Department:	Lamination Department
Analyst:	S. Johnson
Effective Date:	(month/date/year)
Cancels Sheet Dated:	(month/date/year or "None")
Approved by:	(signature)

The job of vinyl laminator involves laminate job planning
and ordering, and cutting and applying vinyl laminate
sheeting to a variety of surfaces including countertops,
doors, and panels with hot and cold adhesives. The work
is conducted on-site and in-plant. It is a skilled job requiring detailed planning, high craftsmanship, and the
use of a variety of power and hand tools to meet customer requirements and quality standards.

Criteria for a Good Job Description

Remember that the job description shows the boundaries of the
job and that the analyst uses a big brush and large strokes. The
four criteria for good job descriptions focus on the title, scope,
form, and length of the description. They are as follows:

Title. A succinct combination of words capturing the overall
job function—more than one word and usually less than
four.

Scope. Embraces the totality of the job and communicates
this by labeling two to seven job functions or clusters
of work activity.

> *Form.* Written in complete sentences — usually one para-
> graph and sometimes two.
> *Length.* A range of twenty-five to seventy-five words.

Writing an acceptable title for a job is usually fairly easy. Making it too general is a common error, however. For example, the
title *supervisor* is too broad; *first-line supervisor* is better. To take
another example, *computer operator* is too general and should
be avoided in favor of a more specific title like *SPSS Software
Consultant.*

Scope is the most difficult criterion to satisfy. The idea of
clustering job functions, rather than listing tasks, requires further discussion. The analyst identifies logical clusters among a
detailed listing of work activities. For instance, it is easy to list
a number of tasks carried out by a restaurant person, such as:

- Preparing tables
- Taking food orders
- Delivering food orders

But what is it that cuts across, or clusters, these individual tasks?
Such behaviors as being friendly, courteous, alert to empty coffee
cups, and attentive to customer needs may at a minimum be
clustered under the words *attentive to customer needs.* *Knowing the menu* and *handling basic billing mathematics* could be
identified as other functions or clusters for this job. Of course,
the job of waitperson will be very different in a neighborhood
diner, a fast-food burger place, or an elegant top-of-the-tower
restaurant. These differences should be reflected in the job
descriptions at the various places of business.

The form and length criteria are easily understood and
should be adhered to. Errors such as making lists rather than
writing sentences, or including too much information, are the
result of the analyst's not paying attention to the criteria. Self-

discipline in writing a good job description now will pay dividends later by providing an accurate framework for specifying the details of the job.

The following is an example of a poor job description. Check it against the four criteria. Do you find any deficiencies?

Job Description

Job or Program:	Supervisor
Location:	Headquarters and Middletown
Department:	Companywide
Analyst:	B. Johnson
Effective Date:	(month/date/year)
Cancels Sheet Dated:	(month/date/year or "None")
Approved by:	(signature)

The supervisor is in charge of bottom-line productivity of a work group. More than any other member of the management team, this individual is responsible for translating company goals into reality by meeting production quotas.

The following is an example of a good job description for you to check against the four criteria:

Job Description

Job or Program:	Production Supervisor
Location:	Headquarters and Middletown
Department:	Companywide
Analyst:	B. Johnson
Effective Date:	(month/date/year)
Cancels Sheet Dated:	(month/date/year or "None")
Approved by:	(signature)

The supervisor is responsible for effective and efficient accomplishment of work within his or her realm of authority. The supervisor understands, supports, and delivers the sequential management functions of planning, organizing, staffing, directing, and controlling. On a day-to-day basis, the supervisor engages in problem analysis, decision-making, and communication activities within his or her realm of authority.

The problem analysis, decision-making, and communication activities are primarily focused on the customer's requirements and quality standards.

You can easily see that these two job descriptions for supervisor differ. At first glance, some people might have judged the first description to be acceptable, although it meets none of the criteria of a good job description.

Acme, Inc. – Shipper Job Description

The Acme, Inc. case study presented in Chapter Three provided the initial overview of an organization experiencing performance problems. Chapter Six included a performance improvement proposal—the outcome of a performance diagnosis—for the Acme Shipping Department. Part of the proposal was a decision to solidify the job of shipper and to train all the incumbents. Here is the description of the position of shipper in Acme's Shipping Department.

Job Description

Job or Program:	Shipper
Location:	St. Paul, Minn.
Department:	Shipping Department
Analyst:	R. Torraco
Effective Date:	(month/date/year)
Cancels Sheet Dated:	(month/date/year or "None")
Approved by:	(signature)

The shipper is responsible for accurately selecting, packing, and loading seat covers for shipment in response to customer orders. Within the Acme, Inc. system of sales, production, distribution, and inventory control, the shipper uses systems data to process and ship customer orders. The shipper also monitors and maintains efficient shipping operations.

Volatile Jobs

Not long ago, a job was likely to be stable. Even if job incumbents changed, the job remained relatively constant. Thus, job descriptions by themselves were important, steady targets. This is no longer the case; organizations and jobs in organizations are more fluid than ever. In fact, it appears today as though jobs are more fluid than the tasks that make up an individual job. With continuing organizational restructuring, stable jobs come and go. At the same time, the tasks remain and are reshuffled into new jobs.

Thus, job descriptions have less organizational utility than in the past. Previously, job descriptions were part of the way an organization was vertically defined—jobs having been connected to organizational functions. Today, we take a systems and process view of the organization. This horizontal process view dictates worker tasks that end up being pragmatically clustered into jobs.

Checkpoint

Take about five minutes to write a job description of either your present job or a past job. If you prefer, use the job description form provided in the Appendix and write a job description that meets the four criteria of title, scope, form, and length. Because you will be making a task inventory next, limit the length of your job description to twenty-five to seventy-five words and the scope to two to seven functions or clusters of work activity. Check your job description against the criteria and the good examples to see if it meets the criteria.

Conclusion

Job descriptions for the purpose of maintaining and improving performance take seriously the idea of defining what people actually do in their jobs, not focusing on hiring prerequisites. The identification of the job functions begins to paint a picture of expertise. The task inventory and the analysis of those tasks fill in the picture and may suggest job description revisions. In the next chapter, I describe the process for producing task inventories.

Chapter 10

Developing
Task Inventories

Most jobs consist of a variety of fairly discrete activities or tasks. Even jobs that first appear to be one dimensional usually become more complex on closer inspection. Take, for example, the job of violinist. At first glance, this job appears to be one dimensional: playing the violin. A closer look, however, yields a list of discrete tasks such as violin maintenance, music procurement, performance scheduling, practicing, and performing. A *task inventory* is a list of the discrete activities—such as those just listed—that make up a specific job in a specific organization.

Developing a Task Inventory

With the criteria for a good task inventory in hand, the task inventory process has four steps (Figure 10.1). It starts with two data collection steps: obtaining existing task inventories and interviewing experts. The advice given to you for job descriptions in the previous chapter applies equally to producing the task inventory. Also, the data for both the job description and the task inventory can be collected at the same time. Again, as with job descriptions, the important steps of drafting and then reviewing and approving the task inventory are presented. The task

Figure 10.1. Developing a Task Inventory.

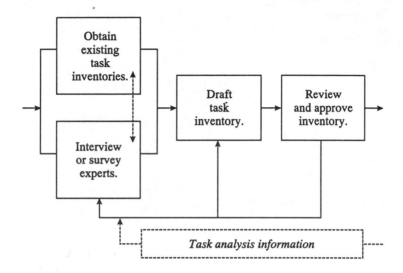

inventory documentation form, which records the output of the process, is found in the Appendix.

As each task is individually analyzed at a later time, the insights derived from that more detailed analysis will likely suggest revisions to the task inventory and possibly the job description.

Criteria for a Good Task Inventory

The four criteria for a good task inventory pertain both to the inventory as a whole and to each task statement in the inventory. The criteria are as follows:

Comprehensive. All work activity fits into one of the inventoried tasks.

Intermediate. A task unit of work activity is intermediate in specificity between that of the job cluster or function and that of a step-by-step procedure or detailed aspect of the job.

Discrete. Each task is distinguishable from the others and has a definite beginning and ending.

Active. Each task statement contains an action verb and the object of the action.

Describing tasks so that they meet the first three criteria—being comprehensive, intermediate, and discrete—is like cutting out a toddler's jigsaw puzzle. The goal is to cut the work into fairly big pieces—pieces that do not overlap but that logically fit together to form a complete picture. The size of the units and the pattern of the pieces will vary from analyst to analyst. The size of the units of work specified at the task inventory level may also vary between companies or departments within companies or between work groups. Take, for example, the nuclear power industry. Here you will find that the technical production people classify job tasks in much smaller units than do their counterparts on the management side. I recognize that analysts are not always comfortable with this variability; common sense should be the arbiter.

The fourth criterion, emphasizing the active nature of the task, connects the work behavior to the object of the work. For a task inventory item, the word *supervises* is too large in scope. Furthermore, it does not meet the active criterion of naming the action and the object being acted on. "Supervises employees" satisfies the requirement of indicating the action and the object. This item still may not be discrete enough, however. For example, such tasks as *supervises sales personnel* and *supervises office personnel* most likely will require work activities and therefore should be listed separately. "Repairing machinery" is appropriate language for a job cluster in a job description, but it is not specific enough to be useful at the task inventory level. "Repairing production-robot grippers" and "replacing milling machine cutting tools" both meet the criteria for a task inventory statement.

Including too much detail in the task statement can also be a problem. The details of job skills should not appear in a task inventory. The full range of specificity is as follows:

1. "Repair machinery" is too general for a task inventory statement, though good for a job description.

2. "Repair production-robot grippers" is just right for a task inventory statement.

3.   "Repair production-robot pneumatic tube #2" is too spe-
     cific for a task inventory statement but would be fine as
     part of a task detail.

Checkpoint

*Now it is your turn to judge the following statements. Place a
"T" next to the items that meet the four criteria of a reasonable
task inventory statement. Some of the items are too general; they
belong in a job description. Some are too specific; they are procedural steps.*

___ *1. Sign purchase orders.*
___ *2. Develop a roll of film.*
___ *3. Repair machinery.*
___ *4. Order back-up supplies.*
___ *5. Direct department work flow.*
___ *6. Obtain stock price quotation.*
___ *7. Remove a molded part from its mold.*
___ *8. Ring up a sale on a cash register.*
___ *9. Analyze and report data.*
___*10. Patch an automobile muffler.*
___*11. Print pictures from an exposed roll of film.*
___*12. Conduct a market analysis.*
___*13. Return customer calls.*
___*14. Schedule worker vacations.*
___*15. Check final product quality against standards.*

*Let's work through your answers one by one. Naturally, we recog-
nize that you are missing some important situational information
that could cause one reader to answer* task, *another to answer*
job, *and still another to answer* task detail *(small step of performing a task), all for the same item. For example, signing a purchase
order is, in most work, a small procedural step. Purchasing floor-*

maintenance equipment could reasonably be labeled a task statement, and signing purchase orders a procedural step. Yet signing
purchase orders in a particular purchasing job that entails a complex process of purchase approvals could be elevated to the task
level. A situation of this nature would rarely occur, but you find
this out for sure by going through the analysis with an expert job
holder. Here are my answers.

Activity	Reasonable First- and Second-Choice Answers
1. Sign purchase orders.	Task detail, task
2. Develop a role of film.	Task, task detail
3. Repair machinery.	Job, task
4. Order back-up supplies.	Task, task detail
5. Direct department work flow.	Task, job
6. Obtain stock price quotation.	Task detail, task
7. Remove a molder part from its mold.	Task detail, task
8. Ring up a sale on a cash register.	Task detail, task
9. Analyze and report data.	Task, job
10. Patch an automobile muffler.	Task, task detail
11. Print pictures from an exposed roll of film.	Task, task detail
12. Conduct a market analysis.	Task, job
13. Return customer calls.	Task detail, task
14. Schedule worker vacations.	Task, task detail
15. Check final product quality against standards.	Task, job

Now, how do you produce a task inventory? There are two approaches, which we will call *bottom-up* and *top-down*. The bottom-up approach requires extensive observation and study of the activities and detailed knowledge required of a worker. The analyst gathers the details and clusters them on the basis of natural breaks or separate categories of activity. The clusters are then labeled and turned into task statements. In the top-down approach, the analyst starts with an existing or newly written job description and then interviews the job holders and their supervisors. The analyst ask questions about the nature of the work, the kinds of activities required, and the amount of time spent on each. Asking how time is spent on the job helps the job holder to consider all the tasks, not just the most obvious ones. This method of self-reporting produces a fairly accurate task inventory with a minimal investment of time. Gathering the details of a specific work behavior by observing the performer at work results in a much greater level of understanding of the task than does eliciting details through interviews. New clusters of details and new perceptions of tasks will likely be identified through observation. Therefore, a task inventory produced in the top-down manner will usually be revised after the detailed task analysis is performed.

Do you remember the job description for the vinyl laminator in Chapter Nine? The task inventory for this job is as follows:

Task Inventory

Job or Program:	Vinyl Laminator
Location:	Custom Kitchens, Inc.
Department:	Lamination Department
Analyst:	S. Johnson
Effective Date:	(month/date/year)
Cancels Sheet Dated:	(month/date/year or "None")
Approved by:	(signature)

Tasks

1. Develop work order plans.
2. Estimate and order materials.

3. Set up work site.
4. Cut laminates to size.
5. Apply laminates.
6. Apply adhesives.
7. Trim laminates.
8. Inspect and protect finished products.
9. Clean up work area.

Acme, Inc. — Task Inventory for the Job of Shipper

The Acme, Inc. case study presented in Chapter Three provided a brief picture of an organization suffering from performance problems. In Chapter Six, we saw an example of a performance improvement proposal for the Acme Shipping Department. Among other things, the proposal reflected a decision to solidify the job of shipper and to train all the incumbents in this position. The description of the job of shipper was presented in Chapter Nine. The following is the task inventory for this job.

Task Inventory

Job or Program: Shipper
Location: St. Paul, Minn.
Department: Shipping Department
Analyst: R. Torraco
Effective Date: (month/date/year)
Cancels Sheet Dated: (month/date/year or "None")
Approved by: (signature)

Tasks

1. Prepare seat cover order.
2. Process seat cover order.
3. Pack and load seat cover order.
4. Monitor and troubleshoot shipping operations.
5. Communicate order status to customers.
6. Perform as shipping team member.
7. Clean Shipping Department.

Each task from the task inventory is analyzed and documented with one or more of the three task analysis tools: procedural task analysis, systems task analysis, or knowledge task analysis. *Procedural* tasks are made up of step-by-step, people-thing work behaviors. *Systems* tasks are made up of people-hardware systems or people-knowledge work behaviors. *Knowledge* tasks are made up of people-idea and people-people work behaviors. Identification of the appropriate task analysis tool (or tools) for each task should become part of the task inventory. For example, the first task—"Prepare seat cover order"—is best analyzed using the procedural task analysis method and should be coded as such. Please review the appropriate task analysis coding for the shipper job tasks on the following task inventory. Very rarely is a job made up of tasks that are all of one type. The job of shipper has seven tasks—four procedural, one systems, and two knowledge.

One more important point is that *some tasks can be cross-functional*. While the first three shipper tasks are sequential, "Monitor and troubleshoot shipping operations" (task 4) cuts across all the other tasks. In a similar way, "Perform as shipping team member" (task 6) cuts across all the tasks. The analyst makes the decision if the work behaviors are embedded with tasks or if they are pervasive enough to justify their own status as a task.

Task Inventory

Job or Program:	Shipper
Location:	St. Paul, Minn.
Department:	Shipping Department
Analyst:	R. Torraco
Effective Date:	(month/date/year)
Cancels Sheet Dated:	(month/date/year or "None")
Approved by:	(signature)

Tasks	*Task Analysis Plan*
1. Prepare seat cover order.	Procedure
2. Process seat cover order.	Procedure

3. Pack and load seat cover order.   Procedure
4. Monitor and troubleshoot shipping operations.   Systems
5. Communicate order status to customers.   Knowledge
6. Perform as shipping team member.   Knowledge
7. Clean Shipping Department.   Procedure

Checkpoint

In Chapter Nine, you wrote your own job description. Now, using the method of self-reporting, construct a task inventory for your job. If you like, you can use the task inventory form in the Appendix. Because you will need this task inventory to do an exercise in a later chapter, it is important that you complete it and that it meets the four criteria of being: (1) comprehensive, (2) intermediate, (3) discrete, and (4) active. In this instance, you are both the analyst and the subject expert. On the job, there will be two of you. The next step is to evaluate your task inventory using the four criteria. Rate your success in complying with each criterion and write four statements about how your task inventory performance measured up.

Job Title: _____

Task Inventory Criteria	Success	Comments
Comprehensive? *All work activity fits into one of the inventoried tasks.*	____Yes ____No	
Intermediate? *The task unit or work activity is intermediate in specificity*	____All ____Some ____None	

*between that of the job cluster
or function and that of a
step-by-step procedure or
detailed aspect of the job.*

Discrete?	____All
Each task is distinguishable	____Some
from the others and has a	____None
definite beginning and ending.	

Active?	____All
Each task statement has an	____Some
action verb and the object of	____None
the action.	

*Chances are, if you experienced difficulty in meeting one
of the criteria, it was the core activity or intermediate criterion.
Finding the right level of specificity takes practice. The concept
of task detailing versus task identification will be clarified in the
next chapter. After you learn more about detailed task analysis
in Chapters Eleven to Thirteen, you can come back to this point
and revise your task inventory as needed.*

Tips for the Analyst

Thus far, work expertise has been documented at two levels:
job description and task inventory. But when a job is simple and
the tasks are limited, it may be reasonable to include the task
inventory in an expanded job description, rather than to produce
two separate documents.

Should the analyst use the job descriptions and task inventories that already exist in the organization? By all means procure these documents. You will find them filed in the human resource department, training department, or industrial engineering department. Be sure to question the relevance of these documents to your task. Are they current or are they outdated? For what purpose were they produced? Hiring? Training? Who wrote them? The incumbent? The supervisor? An analyst? Are they accurate? You may discover that these job descriptions fit the criteria for job descriptions and task inventories and that they may be used as is. More likely, you will find that they are outdated and were written for purposes of hiring or compensation.

At least two people become involved in producing the job description and task inventory. These are the analyst and the subject expert. The most likely subject experts are the job holders and their direct supervisors. Your interviews with these people can be complemented with existing job descriptions, task inventories, job performance aids, and training manuals.

While subject experts are a critical resource in producing quality general work analyses, the skill of the analyst in asking the right questions — the "dumb" questions, the leading questions, the insightful questions — is equally important. Experts, by definition, are so competent that they use their subconscious minds to perform work behaviors. At the conscious level, they can't necessarily recall the detailed work that they take for granted. Supervisors can be either more or less aware of the details of the work than are those they supervise. The skilled analyst brings to the analysis task clear criteria, an inquisitive mind, and a willingness to seek the knowledge of the subject experts — a good combination for documenting work expertise.

Conclusion

Task inventories have enormous utility for performance improvement professionals. They are critical in bridging between the organizational, process, and individual levels of performance. Tasks are fundamentally connected to organizational and process level performance requirements. Even so, jobs are most often designed in terms of how the tasks fit one another rather than how the tasks relate to the organization and its processes.

The next three chapters will show you how to use additional expertise documentation tools. These more precise tools are used to analyze and document what a person needs to know and be able to do to perform specific job tasks. Three task analysis tools will be presented: procedural task analysis, systems task analysis, and knowledge task analysis. All three documentation tools are not always needed to analyze each task. Most tasks can be analyzed by using just one of these tools. Some require more. In general, one task of a job will require one task analysis tool, and a second task will require one of the other task analysis tools. In the next chapter, I describe the process for analyzing procedural tasks — the tool for analyzing people-thing workplace expertise.

Procedural
Task Analysis

Procedural task analysis is a method of documenting people-thing workplace expertise in terms of precisely what people are required to know and be able to do to perform the task. The following small incident demonstrates the important principles, elements, and uses of procedural task analysis.

You Can't Miss It!

A group of executives flew into a metropolitan area for a head-quarters-sponsored seminar. Knowing only that their hotel was located on Park Street, they called from the airport for directions. The hotel clerk told them, "Head north from the airport on Grand Avenue. Cross over Route 28. Turn left on Park. Look for the Holly Hotel on the right side of the road. *You can't miss it!*"

The seminar group followed the instructions carefully and got thoroughly lost. It's ironic that the first topic on the seminar agenda was communication skills!

The explanation for the mix-up seemed simple. Years ago, north-south Park Street had been bisected by the new east-west Route 28. Because no overpass had been provided for, Park

Street was curved to parallel Route 28 until it joined Grand Avenue. The few blocks that parallel Route 28 are called Frontage Road. Yet the hotel staff call it Park Street, which to them it is.

Sometimes the "obvious" is not obvious. You too have probably given or received concise, confident, and wrong directions capped with a "you can't miss it!"

Later that day, the seminar leader asked if the hotel clerk could show her how to get to the Holly Hotel from the airport. She wanted to prevent future embarrassments, and he agreed. The seminar leader hopped into the car with the volunteer expert at the wheel, and off they went. The seminar leader–turned–analyst asked questions and watched landmarks pass by as they traveled. She asked questions such as the following: "Why did you turn here?" "What is the name of this street?" "Is this road heading due north?" "Have you ever gotten lost?" The expert responded and drove while the analyst listened, observed, questioned, and wrote. One result of this exercise was an accurate map. Another was an awareness of the value of having the expert *actually perform the work* as the analyst asked key questions.

Elements of Procedural Task Analysis

A significant proportion of the knowledge and skill required to perform in the workplace is procedural; that is, the work involves people-thing interactions such as filling out forms, operating machines, using tools, and handling goods. Procedural task analysis is the method to use for documenting work performed in a series of steps. Because *all* the steps to complete a task are documented, a procedure analysis document may run to many pages. If all the tasks on an inventory for a specific job are people-thing interactions, a procedural task analysis should be developed for each task. If fifteen such tasks were listed for a job, fifteen separate documents should be on file.

Developing a procedural task analysis typically requires two people: the subject expert and the analyst. An alternative is to teach the procedural task analysis process to subject experts so they can document their own tasks. That the subject expert actually performs the work is another requirement. Simply talking about the work without actually performing it, as did the hotel clerk who gave directions over the telephone, is likely to result in a procedure that drops workers off someplace else or gets them lost. Being accurate and being complete are critical. Without directly observing the work, the analyst is likely to leave several important steps or pieces of information out of the analysis.

The analyst must record the precise details of the work task: the type and size of the wrench, the direction to turn the bolt, how far, and so on. Getting ready to do a procedural task analysis is easy; only a clipboard, a paper pad, and a pencil are required. An instant camera is recommended (or a higher-quality camera if you are working in the field). But first it may be useful to look at the process of procedural task analysis and the documentation form on which to record the analysis.

Process of Analyzing Procedural Tasks

The process of documenting procedural tasks is portrayed in Figure 11.1. The process requires attention to detail: judging the appropriateness of procedural analysis to the job task, honoring the criteria, obtaining existing task analysis documents from inside or outside the organization, observing expert(s) actually performing the task while recording data, and drafting a task analysis document for review and approval.

The final version of a procedural task analysis is recorded on special forms (see the Appendix). The procedural task analysis document is a multipage form, with the first page containing administrative, safety, and other essential information, along with the initial procedural steps necessary to perform the task. The second page is a continuation sheet that is used repeatedly until all the details of the procedure have been recorded. Exhibit 11.1 is an example of the first page of the procedural analysis for the analyst's job task of developing a procedural analysis.

Figure 11.1. Analyzing Procedural Tasks.

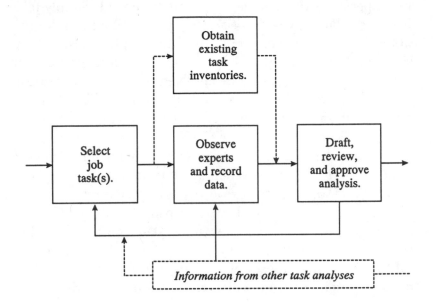

Heading

The top section of the first page of the form (see Exhibit 11.1) contains some of the who, what, when, and where reference information that becomes more valuable as time passes and the analyst's memory fades. It also contains the information needed to maintain complete and up-to-date files. In this instance, the form is simply page 1 of 1. In most instances, it would be reasonable to use many pages in detailing a single task. A set of five pages will be numbered as follows: page 1 of 5, 2 of 5, and so on.

The specific *location* is important in that the work systems in one site could be unique. The fact that the work was analyzed in the Philadelphia or Minneapolis office could be essential information; in some companies, the *department* name could be essential information. For current reference and for a long-term historical perspective, the job or program for which the analysis is being conducted should be recorded. This is important because any analysis work is colored by the purpose for

Exhibit 11.1. Example of First Page
of Procedural Task Analysis Form.

Procedural Task Analysis

Job or Program __Procedural Task Analysis__		Page __1__ Of __1__
Location __Minneapolis__	Effective Date	__1/1/96__
Department __Human Resources__	Cancels Sheet Dated	__None__
Analyst __R.A. Swanson__	Approved By	__D.Gradous__

Task
The task name, taken from the task inventory

Performance Standard
The end-result work performance standard for this task

Safety and Other Cautions
Safety precautions (e.g. wear safety glasses, fragile equipment, etc.)

Major Headings	Sub Headings	Sequential Steps in Performing the Work	Notes*
1.		Short statements on the performance of a task—begin with action words.	C–M
2.		Put these in the 1st order heading column. Begin writing in the column to shape an outline form.	C–M
	A.	Second order headings are key points, or explanations, which further describe the step.	C–M
	B.	These 2nd order headings begin just right of the column.	C–E
	C.	If you use "A," you must use "B."	C–E
3.		Notes column: To identify a learning domain or a particularly difficult task or "skill."	C–D
	A.	Dominant learning domain: Cognitive, Affective, or Psychomotor.	C–D
	B.	Learning difficulty: Easy, Moderate, or Difficult.	C–M

*Learning Domain: Cognitive = C. Affective = A. Psychomotor = P.   *Learning Difficulty: Easy = E. Moderate = M. Difficult = D.

which it is done. For example, the technical know-how required of salespeople will differ greatly from that required of the service-and-repair people who deal with the same product. The substance of the organizational diagnosis and the resulting performance improvement proposal (see Chapter Six) should have already made this clear. In addition, the Taxonomy of Performance (see Figure 5.7) helps the analyst continually differentiate the true nature and level of detail required of the procedural task being documented.

In addition to the *effective date* or the date that the procedural analysis is completed and approved, the *cancels sheet dated* line in our example indicates that this is an updated version of the procedure. And finally, recording the name of the *analyst* and *approved by* enhances accountability and future communications.

The next section of the first page, *task*, is the place to write a single task name and number from the task inventory. The identical number and words used to specify the task in the inventory should be repeated here. For example, the "Repair production-robot grippers" task example from Chapter Ten would be entered on the earlier task inventory form *and* on the procedural task analysis form. Next is the section for recording the performance standard for this task. The performance standard for the robot gripper is as follows: "The technician is able to remove worn grippers, install new grippers, and adjust them to $+/-$ .0001 in less than 30 minutes."

The final section at the top of the form offers space for recording cautionary items about safety and other essential points that should be highlighted. "Must wear safety glasses" and "Use heat-resistant gloves" are a few examples of items that could be entered here.

Sequential Steps

The sequential steps for a procedure are written in the form of short statements describing the actual performance of a task. Each statement begins with an action word like *turn, listen, fill, set,* or *compare.* Here is a sample statement for setting air pressure on a production machine: "Set forming pressure to 30 to 35 pounds per square inch (psi)."

Procedural information is usually broken down into headings and subheadings. For example, setting forming pressure requires several discrete activities. In this instance, subheadings would be as follows:

A. Depress the "inflate form" button and hold.
B. Set forming pressure to 30 to 35 pounds per square inch (psi).
C. Release the "inflate form" button.

The *notes* column on the procedural task analysis form allows space for recording vital information about the *learning domain* and the estimated *difficulty* of learning each procedural detail. Almost any work performance calls on a mix of cognitive (intellectual), affective (attitudinal), and psychomotor (sensory) domains. Procedural work rarely calls on just a single domain. Rather, one of the three domains is dominant. The question to ask is this: "Are the differences between workers who are expert and those who are beginners primarily the result of knowing or not knowing something, having or not having certain attitudes, or being able or unable to make fine sensory discriminations?" The answer will sometimes surprise the analyst.

Consider the following example. A skilled worker casually rubs a hand over a finely finished part and decides to stop and redo the work. You, in the role of the analyst, ask what the worker is doing. You rub your hand over the same part and feel nothing unusual. A little knowledge and the ability to make some fine sensory discriminations, developed over years of experience, are at work here. This activity is psychomotor and is therefore coded *P.* Other psychomotor activities may include using fine discrimination with any of the senses of sight, smell, taste, hearing, and touch. In another instance, a skilled worker moves rapidly through a series of assembly and adjustment procedures—

all of which appear to be psychomotor behaviors but in fact are not. Anyone with reasonable psychomotor control could push the parts in place, turn the adjusting knobs, trip the start lever, turn the finished part, and so on. The worker's cognitive ability to remember many sequential steps allows for speed in this procedure. This activity is coded C.

By asking questions about how one could perform the work improperly or by trying to do the task yourself, or both, you can determine the learning domain.

Deciding how difficult a step is to learn is another matter. Be sure to make such judgments while you are close to the work. Having this information will help at a later time when you are trying to understand why workers are either bored or getting stuck in the learning-working process and how you should respond. If you are a trainer, you may decide to offer additional practice time during training for difficult-to-learn tasks. If you are a manager, you may want to redesign a boring task to make the work more challenging. But for now, the analyst's responsibility is to rate each sequential step in terms of learning domain and learning difficulty.

Now let's look at a completed procedural analysis for a simple task, making a telephone call (see Exhibit 11.2). Take time to read this example carefully so you can see the level of detail specified.

It is important that you note the level of detail. Variations among procedural analyses usually are found in the amount of detail cited in the sequential steps. Most beginning analysts do not include enough detail. A second area of significant difference will usually appear in the *notes* column, with the analyst misclassifying cognitive work as psychomotor work. Take heart! Experience will reduce these differences as you become a more practiced analyst.

Did you notice that a drawing of a telephone was added to the procedural analysis for making a telephone call? Do you recall the efforts to produce an accurate map for getting from the metropolitan airport to the Holly Hotel? Sketches, photographs, and existing diagrams of equipment are critical additions to most procedural analyses. A sketchpad, a photocopier, and an instant camera are essential elements of the analyst's support equipment.

Checkpoint

While you may not be ready to do a procedural task analysis, you should be able to begin. To test your skills, complete the analysis and documentation of the telephone-calling task by adding the sequential steps required for "automatic redialing." This work task detail is an immediate follow-up to a dialed telephone number that was busy. Add these details to the end of Exhibit 11.2. Remember that the procedural analysis criteria include:

1. *Writing short statements of the performance*

2. *Beginning with action words*

3. *Using headings and subheadings*

4. *Identifying the learning domain and the level of learning difficulty for each step*

Blow Molder Operator:
Analyzing Procedural Tasks

To help you put the parts of a procedural analysis together, this chapter includes actual, complete analysis of the procedural tasks of the blow molder operator. The blow molder is a production machine for making such hollow plastic objects as bottles, toys, and coin banks. By using heat and air, it converts plastic pellets into formed objects. The plastic pellets are fed into the machine and melted. Then molten plastic is extruded in the form of a soft plastic tubing, which is then captured inside a two-piece

Exhibit 11.2. Procedural Analysis for Making a Telephone Call.

Procedural Task Analysis

Job or Program __Telephone Equipment__		Page _1_ Of _2_
Location _____South-East Telephone, Inc.__	Effective Date _____10/2/95_____	
Department _____Customer Service_____	Cancels Sheet Dated __4/4/94__	
Analyst _____G. Poor_____	Approved By _____C. La Bandera_____	

Task
Make a telephone call

Performance Standard
Given a desk-style push-button telephone, and a telephone number, the customer will be able to call time and temperature and respond directly to either a ringing connection or a busy signal.

Safety and Other Cautions
None

Major Headings	Sub Headings	Sequential Steps in Performing the Work	Notes*
1.		Locate standard desk dial telephone (see drawing).	C–E
2.		Pick up the receiver.	C–E
	A.	'C'-shaped component on top of phone.	C–E
	B.	Put mouthpiece (with end cord coming from it) at your mouth and the earpiece at your ear.	C–E
3.		Listen for dial tone (steady buzzing sound coming from earpiece).	P–E
4.		Locate time and temperature telephone number (seven-digit number located in center of dial on phone body.	C–E
5.		Dial phone number.	P–E
	A.	Take 1st number from phone number, find the corresponding number on the keypad, press firmly and quickly release.	P–E
	B.	Repeat step 5A with the second through seventh digit of the telephone number. Then go to step 6.	P–E

*Learning Domain: Cognitive = C. Affective = A. Psychomotor = P.   *Learning Difficulty: Easy = E. Moderate = M. Difficult = D.

Exhibit 11.2. Procedural Analysis for Making a Telephone Call, Cont'd.

Procedural Task Analysis

Task: Make a telephone call   (Continued)

Job or Program __Telephone Equipment__	Page __2__ Of __2__
Location __South-East Telephone, Inc.__	Effective Date __10/2/95__
Department __Customer Service__	Cancels Sheet Dated __4/4/94__
Analyst __G. Poor__	Approved By __C. La Bandera__

Major Headings	Sub Headings	Sequential Steps in Performing the Work	Notes*
6.		Listen for a connection.	P–E
	A.	If you hear an alternate clicking sound (1 second) and silence (2 seconds), wait until you hear a recording of the time and temperature, then go to step 7.	
	B.	If you hear a rapid buzzing sound, it means the line is busy; go to step 7.	P–E
7.		Hang up (replace receiver on hook of base unit).	C–E

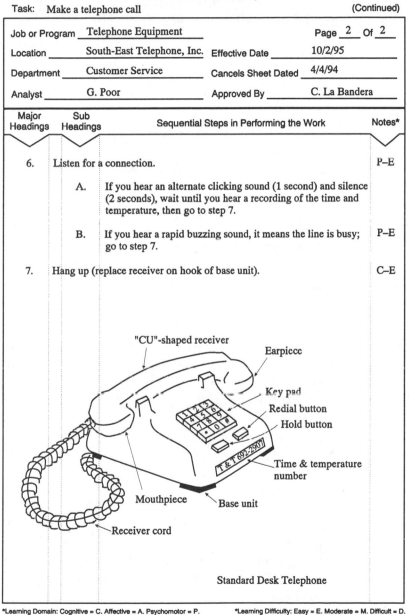

Standard Desk Telephone

*Learning Domain: Cognitive = C. Affective = A. Psychomotor = P.   *Learning Difficulty: Easy = E. Moderate = M. Difficult = D.

mold. The still-soft plastic tubing is filled with air and blown up to conform to the mold. The plastic cools and sets in the shape of the mold. The mold is then opened and the plastic object removed. A description and illustration of the blow molder can be seen in Figure 11.2.

The setup task is the first of three tasks taken from the operator's task inventory:

Blow Molder Operator Task Inventory

1. Set up the blow molder.
2. Operate the blow molder.
3. Shut down the blow molder.

Exhibit 11.3 contains a procedural analysis for each of these tasks. Read the procedural analysis in this exhibit carefully. To test your understanding, answer the questions that follow.

Checkpoint

Answering the following six questions will permit you to assess your understanding of the setup procedure for the blow molder. Use the procedural analysis in Exhibit 11.3. Compare your answers with mine at the end of this chapter.

Procedural Task Analysis Questions on the Blow Molder

__1. *To operate the blow molder primarily requires_____ behavior.*
   a. *cognitive*
   b. *affective*
   c. *psychomotor*
__2. *The drawing portion of the blow molder procedural task analysis is_____.*
   a. *not necessary*
   b. *a nice addition*
   c. *crucial*

Figure 11.2. Blow Molder.

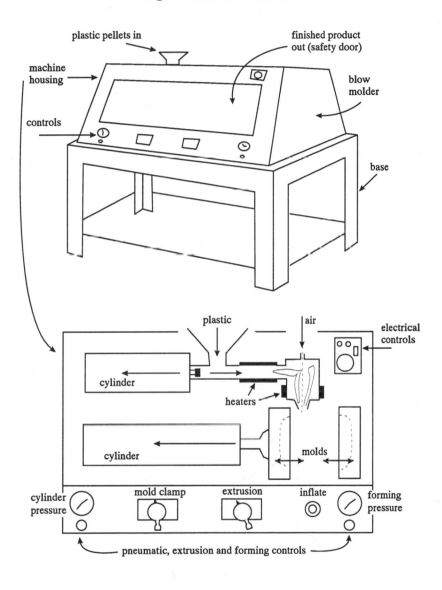

Exhibit 11.3. Procedural Analyses of the Setup,
Operation, and Shutdown of the Blow Molder.

Procedural Task Analysis

Job or Program	Blow molder operator		Page 1 Of 3
Location	Twin-Cities Plastic	Effective Date	12/10/95
Department	Production	Cancels Sheet Dated	3/24/93
Analyst	J. Martelli	Approved By	C. Bishop

Task Set up the Blow Molder

Performance Standard
The operator will set up the blow molder for production of banks with the air pressure and temperature within tolerances.

Safety and Other Cautions
1. Machine becomes hot while setting up.
2. Wear safety glasses.

Major Headings	Sub Headings	Sequential Steps in Performing the Work	Notes*
1.		Connect power plug to a 110 V.A.C. power source.	C–E
2.		Turn power switch "on."	C–E
	A.	Power and heater light will glow.	C–E
	B.	Allow 15-20 minutes for warm-up.	C–E
3.		Connect air supply to intake connection.	
	A.	Located on left side of machine.	C–E
	B.	Pull back on air connector while pushing into the machine air intake connection (located on rear left side of machine).	P–M
4.		Place funnel in top of the molder.	P–E
	A.	Opening for the funnel is in center on the top surface of the molder.	P–E
	B.	Insure that the funnel is properly seated in the feed hopper.	P–E
5.		Fill funnel with polyethelene pellets.	C–E
	A.	Add the pellets slowly to avoid plugging the hopper.	P–E

*Learning Domain: Cognitive = C. Affective = A. Psychomotor = P.   *Learning Difficulty: Easy = E. Moderate = M. Difficult = D.

Exhibit 11.3. Procedural Analyses of the Setup, Operation, and Shutdown of the Blow Molder, Cont'd.

Procedural Task Analysis

Task: Set up the Blow Molder (Continued)

Job or Program Blow molder operator		Page 2 Of 3
Location Twin-Cities Plastic	Effective Date	12/10/95
Department Production	Cancels Sheet Dated 3/24/93	
Analyst J. Martelli	Approved By	C. Bishop

Major Headings	Sub Headings	Sequential Steps in Performing the Work	Notes*
	B.	Fill funnel 5/8 full.	C-E
6.		Set cylinder pressure to 74-95 lbs.	C/P-E
	A.	Place "hold clamp" lever in "open" position and hold.	P-E
	B.	Turn black dial under cylinder pressure valve until the gauge above it reads 75-95 lbs.	C/P-E
7.		Set "forming pressure" to 30-35 lbs.	C/P-E
	A.	Depress the "inflate form" button and hold.	C-E
	B.	Turn black knob under forming pressure gauge until the gauge reads 30-35 lbs.	C/P-E
	C.	Release "inflate form" button.	C-E
8.		Set molding temperature to 350-400° F.	C-M
	A.	Read temperature gauge in left side of power switch.	C-E
	B.	If temperature is under 350° and heater light is on, wait until temperature light goes off, then continue with 8C.	C-E
	C.	If temp. is under 350° and heater light is off, go to 9.	C-E
	D.	If temp. is over 400° and heater light is on or off, go to 10.	C-E
	E.	If temp. is between 350° and 400° and heater light is off, ready for production.	C-E
9.		Set temp. up to 350-400°.	C/P-M
	A.	Place a flat blade screwdriver in hole by upper left corner of temp. gauge.	P-M
	B.	Slowly turn temperature set-screw *clockwise* until heater light comes on; the more you turn, the more the temp. will increase.	P-D
	C.	Wait until heater light goes off.	C-E
	D.	If temp. is under 350°, repeat 9A-D until 350°-400° is reached with heater light off.	C/P-M

*Learning Domain: Cognitive = C. Affective = A. Psychomotor = P.   *Learning Difficulty: Easy = E. Moderate = M. Difficult = D.

Exhibit 11.3. Procedural Analyses of the Setup,
Operation, and Shutdown of the Blow Molder, Cont'd.

Procedural Task Analysis

Task: Set up the Blow Molder   (Continued)

Job or Program	Blow molder operator		Page 3 Of 3
Location	Twin-Cities Plastic	Effective Date	12/10/95
Department	Production	Cancels Sheet Dated	3/24/93
Analyst	J. Martelli	Approved By	C. Bishop

Major Headings	Sub Headings	Sequential Steps in Performing the Work	Notes*
10.		Set temp. down to 350-400°.	C/P-M
	A.	Place a flat blade screwdriver in the hole by upper left corner of the temp. gauge.	P-M
	B.	Slowly turn the temperature set-screw *counter clockwise* until heater light goes off; the more you turn, the lower the temp. will drop.	P-D
	C.	Wait for temp. to drop and stabilize for one minute.	C-E
	D.	If temp. is above 400°, repeat 10A-D.	
	E.	If temp. is below 350°, repeat 9A-D.	
	F.	When temp. is between 350-400°, machine is ready for production.	C-E

*Learning Domain: Cognitive - C. Affective - A. Psychomotor - P.   *Learning Difficulty: Easy - E. Moderate - M. Difficult - D.

Exhibit 11.3. Procedural Analyses of the Setup,
Operation, and Shutdown of the Blow Molder, Cont'd.

Procedural Task Analysis

Job or Program __Blow molder operator__	Page _1_ Of _2_
Location __Twin-Cities Plastic__	Effective Date __12/10/95__
Department __Production__	Cancels Sheet Dated __3/24/94__
Analyst __J. Martelli__	Approved By __C. Bishop__

Task
Operate the Blow Molder

Performance Standard
The operator will produce acceptable quality banks at the estab-lished rate.

Safety and Other Cautions
Machine is hot during operation—avoid touching hot surfaces.
Wear safety glasses and heat resistant glove on one hand.

Major Headings	Sub Headings	Sequential Steps in Performing the Work	Notes*
1.		Untrap feed hopper (sucking sound if plastic pellets are trapped).	P-E
	A.	Obtain "ramrod" (dowel rod).	C-E
	B.	Place end in funnel and gently push up and down in funnel/hopper.	P-E
	C.	This allows any plugging in the funnel to untrap and continue plastic feed.	P-E
2.		Slide plastic door on right side of machine open for access to mold.	C-E
3.		Lubricate mold cavity with silicon spray.	P-M
	A.	Spray both halves.	C-E
	B.	Apply sparingly.	P-M
4.		Close plastic door completely.	C-E
5.		Extrude parison from machine (hot plastic sleeve squeezing out of die).	C/P-M
	A.	Place extrusion handle in "feed" position and hold.	C/P-E
	B.	Observe parison extruding from the die (small metal ring forming the parison) between the mold.	P-M

*Learning Domain: Cognitive = C. Affective = A. Psychomotor = P.   *Learning Difficulty: Easy = E. Moderate = M. Difficult = D.

Exhibit 11.3. Procedural Analyses of the Setup, Operation, and Shutdown of the Blow Molder, Cont'd.

Procedural Task Analysis

Task: Operate the Blow Molder (Continued)

Job or Program	Blow molder operator		Page 2 Of 2
Location	Twin-Cities Plastic	Effective Date	12/10/95
Department	Production	Cancels Sheet Dated	3/24/94
Analyst	J. Martelli	Approved By	C. Bishop

Major Headings	Sub Headings	Sequential Steps in Performing the Work	Notes*
	C.	When bottom tip of parison reaches bottom of mold, release the extrude handle.	C-M
6.		Place "hold clamp" in close position and wait four seconds.	C/P-E
7.		Form object.	C/P-E
	A.	Depress "inflate form" bottom and hold for 15-20 seconds then release.	C/P-E
	B.	Wait 20 more seconds.	C-E
8.		Turn hold clamp lever to open position.	P-E
9.		Remove the object.	P-E
	A.	Wear glove.	A-E
	B.	Slide plastic door open.	P-E
	C.	Gently grab object with gloved hand.	A-E
	D.	Pull down and twist until object comes off of die.	P-E
10.		Put object in parts bin.	P-E
11.		Fill hopper with P.E. pellets.	P-E
	A.	Fill hopper slowly to avoid jamming hopper.	A-E
	B.	Fill 5/8 full.	P-E
12.		Untrap feed hopper.	P-E
	A.	Obtain ramrod.	C-E
	B.	Place end in funnel and gently push up and down to untrap P.E. material.	P-E
13.		Repeat steps 4-12 to maintain production.	C/P-M

*Learning Domain: Cognitive = C. Affective = A. Psychomotor = P.   *Learning Difficulty: Easy = E. Moderate = M. Difficult = D.

Exhibit 11.3. Procedural Analyses of the Setup,
Operation, and Shutdown of the Blow Molder, Cont'd.

Procedural Task Analysis

Job or Program ___Blow molder operator___	Page _1_ Of _1_
Location ___Twin-Cities Plastic___	Effective Date ___12/10/95___
Department ___Production___	Cancels Sheet Dated ___3/24/94___
Analyst ___J. Martelli___	Approved By ___C. Bishop___

Task
    Shut down of Blow Molder

Performance Standard
    The operator will properly shut down the molder according to department procedures.

Safety and Other Cautions
    Machine is hot—use caution.
    Wear safety glasses.

Major Headings	Sub Headings	Sequential Steps in Performing the Work	Notes*
1.		Remove final part from mold.	P-E
2.		Shut off power switch.	C-E
3.		Release cylinder pressure.	C/P-M
	A.	Place "hold clamp" lever in open position.	C/P-M
	B.	Turn black dial under cylinder pressure valve counter clockwise until pressure reads 0.	P-E
	C.	Release "hold clamp" lever.	P-E
4.		Release forming pressure.	C-E
	A.	Depress "inflate form" button.	C-E
	B.	Turn black knob under forming pressure until valve reads 0.	C-E
	C.	Release button.	C-E
5.		Unplug power cord.	C-E
6.		Disconnect air supply.	P-M
7.		Clean off machine with brush.	A-E

*Learning Domain: Cognitive = C. Affective = A. Psychomotor = P.   *Learning Difficulty: Easy = E. Moderate = M. Difficult = D.

___3. The blow molder uses_____.
   a. electricity
   b. air pressure
   c. electricity and air pressure
___4. The molding temperature set-screw must be_____to raise the temperature.
   a. turned to the right
   b. turned to the left
   c. pressed in
___5. The most complex aspect of setting up the blow molder appears to be_____.
   a. connecting the power sources
   b. setting the temperature
   c. setting the air pressure
___6. The purpose of the funnel is to_____.
   a. feed pellets into the hopper
   b. feed finished products away from the molds
   c. do both a and b

Answers

1.c   2.a   3.c   4.a   5.b   6.a

Acme Inc.—Procedural Task Analysis of Processing Seat Cover Orders

The Acme, Inc. case study presented in Chapter Three provided a glimpse of an organization confronting performance problems. Chapter Six included a performance improvement proposal— the outcome of a performance diagnosis targeting the Acme Shipping Department. Recommendations included revamping the job of shipper and training all the job incumbents. The description of the job of shipper was incorporated in Chapter Nine; the task inventory for this job was presented in Chapter Ten. One of the seven tasks on the inventory was "Process seat cover order" (Task 2). Exhibit 11.4 provides an analysis of that task.

Tips for the Analyst

Procedural analysis is a fairly direct method of analyzing work expertise. In most cases, what you see is what you record. Careful observers usually do a good job of documenting procedural tasks. Those analysts who question skillfully as well as observe will likely succeed. Be aware that the casual behavior of an expert may fool even the most careful observer. The skilled analyst gently probes for what the worker is doing and why. Whenever safe and appropriate, the expert analyst will ask, "May I try doing that?" By experiencing the work, the analyst will either clarify each step or find many new questions to ask about the work. Actually, doing the work often highlights the need for reducing the analysis to finer steps and substeps.

Conclusion

Procedural task analysis, which focuses on people-thing work expertise, is used to describe usual work behaviors under normal conditions. But abnormal conditions are certain to arise at least some of the time. What happens when the blow molder operator experiences production problems? If the machine breaks, the maintenance department will handle the situation. If the machine lacks the capacity to produce the number of parts per hour demanded — or if it is unreliable due to worn parts — management will handle the situation. Assume that the machine is neither worn nor broken but that the product is blemished or poorly formed. Perhaps the machine is sending abnormal messages through its dials and indicators or is emitting an unusual odor. All is not well. In this case, consulting a procedural analysis for normal operation will not be particularly helpful. The operator is facing a systems problem, not a procedural problem.

People-system workplace expertise requires that the operator understand the processes involved in the system and be

Exhibit 11.4. Analysis of a Shipper's Procedural Task.

Procedural Task Analysis

Job or Program	Shipper		Page 1 Of 3
Location	St. Paul, Minn.	Effective Date	1/1/95
Department	Shipping	Cancels Sheet Dated	None
Analyst	R. Torraco	Approved By	Department head

Task

Process seat cover order

Performance Standard

The shipper will process orders accurately (at 95% accuracy or higher) and in a timely manner (30 or more completed orders per day).

Safety and Other Cautions
1. Follow proper lifting procedures.
2. Follow safe lift-truck and cart operation procedures.

Major Headings	Sub Headings	Sequential Steps in Performing the Work	Notes*
1.		Review *Order Ticket* for specifications of the order to be shipped. (See appendix to Procedure Analysis entitled *Order Ticket*.)	C-M
	A.	Note *quantity* of seat covers ordered under "Total Parts Ordered."	C-E
	B.	Note seat cover *fabric* (Three fabric options = Vinyl, Cloth, Deluxe).	C-E
	C.	Note seat cover *style* (Two style options = Bucket Seat, Bench Seat).	C-E
	D.	Note *delivery speed* desired by customer.	C-E
		(1) "Priority" shipment is delivered within 24 hours of order.	
		(2) "Standard" shipment is delivered within 2-3 days of order.	
2.		Obtain supplies and equipment needed to process order.	C-E
	A.	Obtain an adequate number of shipping containers to pack order for shipment.	C-E
	B.	Obtain flatbed cart to transport shipping containers from lower-level part bins.	C-E
	C.	Retain *Order Ticket* and marking pen for use throughout order processing.	C-E
	Note:	Layout of parts inventory is designed to prevent shipper lifting injuries and minimize the mishandling of parts.	
3.		The layout of the inventory in the warehouse is arranged such that the heaviest parts are stored on the lowest warehouse shelves and the lightest parts are on the highest shelves.	C-E
4.		Information on the *Order Ticket* is arranged to match the layout of warehouse inventory (see appendix photos). Parts located together in the warehouse are listed together on the *Order Ticket* (page 3).	C-E

*Learning Domain: Cognitive = C. Affective = A. Psychomotor = P.   *Learning Difficulty: Easy = E. Moderate = M. Difficult = D.

Exhibit 11.4. Analysis of a Shipper's Procedural Task, Cont'd.

Procedural Task Analysis

Task: Process seat cover order   (Continued)

Job or Program __Shipper__		Page __2__ Of __3__
Location __St. Paul, Minn.__	Effective Date ___1/1/95___	
Department __Shipping__	Cancels Sheet Dated __None__	
Analyst __R. Torraco__	Approved By __Department head__	

Major Headings	Sub Headings	Sequential Steps in Performing the Work	Notes*
5.		Select parts from inventory.	
	A.	Select parts by following sequence of parts as listed on *Order Ticket*.	C-E
		(1) Proceed from left to right on *Order Ticket*.	C-E
		(2) Proceed from top to bottom on *Order Ticket*.	C-E
	B.	Locate parts bin that corresponds to part number of seat cover ordered.	P E
	C.	Select part from bin and place it in shipping container.	C/P-E
	D.	Insure that part number of seat cover selected corresponds to customer order.	C-E
	E.	If part ordered by customer is out-of-stock, refer to *Troubleshooting* task analysis.	C-M
	F.	Repeat steps 5.B through 5.E for all parts listed on *Order Ticket*.	C-E
6.		Record the parts selected on the *Order Ticket*.	C-E
	A.	Record exact number of parts selected under "Part No. Shipped—Quantity."	C-E
	B.	Record exact number of parts substituted under "Part No. Substituted—Quantity."	C-E
	C.	Circle any out-of-stock part numbers for which substitution was required.	C-E
7.		Send shipping containers to warehouse loading area.	
	A.	Place shipping containers filled from upper-level shelves on conveyor belt.	P-E
		(1) Activate conveyor belt (if belt is stationary).	C-E
		(2) Press *black* button to start motor and activate motion warning system.	C-E
		(3) Press *green* button to begin conveyor belt movement.	C-E
	B.	Place shipping containers filled from lower-level shelves on flatbed cart.	P-E
	C.	Transport flatbed cart to warehouse loading area.	P-E
8.		Refer to Shipper task analysis *Pack and Load Seat Cover Order* for packing, labeling, final inspection, and loading procedures.	C-E

*Learning Domain: Cognitive = C. Affective = A. Psychomotor = P.   *Learning Difficulty: Easy = E. Moderate = M. Difficult = D.

Exhibit 11.4. Analysis of a Shipper's Procedural Task, Cont'd.

ACME Seat Cover Co.   ACME Seat Cover Co.   ACME Seat Cover Co.   ACME Seat Cover Co.   ACME Seat Cover Co.   ACME Seat Cover Co.

Order Ticket

CUSTOMER DATA

Customer:_____   Customer Tel. No. _____

Customer
Account No._____   Date Order Received:_____

Customer
Address: _____   Order Received By:_____

SHIPPING DATA

Shipping Mode: *Ground Transport*   Date Order Filled:_____
(Circle One)   *Air Transport*
                    International Air
                                                Date Order Shipped:_____
Delivery Carrier: *ACME*
(Circle One)   *UPS*
                    Other   Shipper's Name:_____

Delivery Speed: *Priority* (within 24 hrs)
(Circle One)   *Standard* (within 2-3 days)

ORDER DATA

Part No. Ordered--Quantity   Part No. Substituted--Quantity   Part No. Shipped--Quantity

Total Parts Ordered:_____   Total Parts Shipped:_____

able to troubleshoot the system. Many work procedures that have broken down or are in trouble do not necessarily involve information systems or decision-making systems. Understanding such systems processes and how to troubleshoot failing systems—information systems and hardware systems—is dealt with in the next chapter. Systems task analysis is an essential skill of the performance analyst because he or she must know how to document work expertise that involves systems.

Chapter 12

Systems
Task Analysis

Our world—including the systems designed by people and the objects made by people—is very complicated. The complexity of our work systems, both technical and information based, can stop us in our tracks. Procedural tasks no longer prevail in the workplace. Rather, it is now dominated by systems and systemic work tasks that have become increasingly complex and abstract. Even everyday nonwork systems can illustrate this point:

> A thirteen-year-old boy owns two bicycles. One bike is a twenty-inch, one-speed, fat-tired model that has been with him since age five. The other is a twenty-six-inch, ten-speed, lightweight model he bought two years ago.
>
> The old twenty-inch bike, bulky and simple in design, has been regularly disassembled and reassembled by its owner for a variety of reasons ranging from major overhauls and repainting to taking it apart just for the fun of it. This bike has very few parts; you can almost see how every part fits together and works. Thus, it has posed few problems to the young owner.
>
> The ten-speed model, on the other hand, has never once been disassembled, despite its sitting disabled for long periods of time. The caliper brakes, the two shift-

ing systems, and all those gears and idlers have proved to be too intimidating to its owner.

Time has changed the world in which we and the young bicycle owner live. We used to believe that we understood the world and had things well under control; but now, with changing technologies all around us, we need extra help in coping with the knowledge systems and hardware systems with which we live and work. And they cannot be set aside or ignored.

More often than we realize, the interdependence between the components of even a simple work system can escape experienced workers and result in a system that is out of control, causing wasted time. For example:

> The president of a small service firm was puzzled. Several subscribers to the firm's professional newsletter wrote to her directly—a few even telephoned—to complain that they had failed to receive their issue of the newsletter. Copies of canceled checks and letters of acknowledgment from the firm's subscription clerk confirmed their subscriber status. The president talked to the subscription clerk, who was worrying about her continued employment with the firm. The clerk had checked her records, found the orders and the computer input records, and concluded that she had entered everything correctly. After all, most of the subscribers were getting their newsletters. To those subscribers who complained, the clerk sent her apologies and her assurance that their names would be reentered into the subscriber files.
>
> Meanwhile, the newsletter manager was frustrated over the situation. He contemplated letting the subscription clerk go, but he was afraid of an even greater mess if someone else took over. He couldn't coach her, because he did not know all the components of her job (much less how they should be executed systematically for optimal effectiveness and efficiency). Neither he nor the clerk understood the firm's newsletter work system, much less how to improve it.

At one time, employees worked their way up in an organization and learned the ropes from those who knew the ropes. Knowing the ropes was largely dependent on staying reasonably alert, having a reasonably positive attitude toward working for the company, and having a great deal of experience. Old-timers could then report with great authority on the idiosyncrasies of their company's work methods and the equipment with which they had regularly interacted throughout their working life. Newcomers listened to them and learned.

This serene model of the workplace — which also held true for the front office, the sales force, and the production floor — no longer exists. To deny this truth is to deny the realities of business and industry. For example, today's production and maintenance personnel are as apt to be wearing a white shirt and using a stethoscope as they are to be equipped with coveralls, an oil can, and an assortment of general mechanic's tools. Today's machine operators may be as adept at computer programming as they are at selecting cutting tools. The presence of automated and cybernetic production systems has erased the old stereotypes of how work is done. The high cost of today's equipment has decreased the probability of having backup equipment, which, in turn, has increased the pressures for keeping our high-cost equipment running. *No production* means *no return* on an enormous capital investment.

Similarly, the systems aspects of the work of the knowledge worker have increased in complexity. Financial networks, personnel systems, prescribed decision-making methods, and communication systems in large and dispersed organizations make work more difficult to comprehend. When errors and inefficiencies occur or when record-keeping systems fail, management is often tempted to fire people or to add a tier of supervisory and quality control staff, rather than figure out how the entire system works, how it can malfunction, or how it is being misunderstood.

Because work systems, and the nature of work itself, have changed so drastically in the past several decades, we face a basic problem: How do we keep our costly work systems up and running, let alone improve them? The consequences of not doing so are huge and can usually be expressed in terms of enormous personnel or financial loss. Clearly, people are required to learn and understand the systemic aspects of their work tasks more thoroughly than they have in the past.

Unfortunately, procedural task analysis methods are inadequate for describing many of the essential systemic work tasks required of many employees. The need exists for an analysis method that specifically focuses on the interrelated job tasks required to keep work systems running effectively and efficiently.

As we saw in Chapters Eleven, the results of procedural task analyses are sequential task details—cookbook-style, step-by-step information for normal operating procedures under normal conditions. The expertise workers must have to respond effectively to abnormal conditions is often left to their resourcefulness. As a result, *many workers make a financial decision, process a form, or run a machine purely from a procedural perspective, unaware of how their actions may affect other aspects of the system of which the job tasks are just one part. They never know what is really going on inside the overall system in which they participate.* Unfortunately, the same workers may now be required by their job to have a much deeper understanding of their entire work system and to take charge whenever processes within the system are not operating normally. Even more problematic are the situations where experienced workers fail to diagnose the inoperative, inefficient, or failing systems within which they work simply because they lack systemic task expertise. Systemic tasks, including diagnosing and troubleshooting systems, are critical activities for keeping business and industry productive.

Where does a worker begin to deal with a failure in a complex system? Furthermore, how does the expert troubleshooter document what he or she does on the job, or in the absence of an expert, how are the required systemic tasks (of present or new systems) figured out?

Analyzing Systemic Tasks

Analysis of systemic work is one of three methods that constitute a complete toolbox for analyzing the expertise of job tasks. The other two methods are (1) the analysis of procedural tasks—for step-by-step, people-thing work behavior (see Chapter Eleven)—and (2) the analysis of knowledge tasks, which embrace people-idea and people-people work behaviors (see Chapter Thirteen).

In this chapter, I will first briefly describe the process of analyzing total systems, processes, and systemic tasks—the expertise required to understand and troubleshoot workplace information-based and/or hardware systems. Several examples and explanations will be provided to help you understand the method.

First, let's walk through the steps of analyzing systemic work, as shown in Figure 12.1. As the figure shows, the elements of the systems task analysis method include systems description and flow, systems parts and purposes, process analysis, and troubleshooting analysis. These elements are defined as follows; a more in-depth discussion of each comes later in this chapter.

Figure 12.1. Analyzing Systems Tasks.

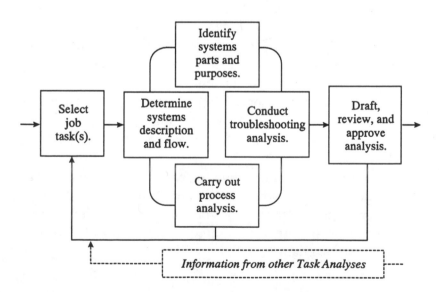

Systems Description and Flow

Naming the system or systemic task being analyzed is important. What it is called begins to bound the analysis. In providing names, it is important to differentiate between a system and a process. A *system* is defined as a unified, purposeful whole consisting of interdependent components or parts. A *process* is a systematic series of actions directed to some defined end.

An *organization* can be viewed as an entire system containing one or more subsystems, or processes, each of which may have a number of subprocesses. The concept of system is generally thought to be broader than the concept of process, and it is used that way in this book. Experts interacting with an entire system almost always require expertise in knowledge tasks, while experts interacting with processes may only require expertise in procedural tasks. However, both increasingly require systemic task workplace behavior.

It is usually not difficult to connect the overall job tasks of a senior executive versus those of a mail handler to a system, subsystem, or process level. The challenge is in framing an individual systemic task at the appropriate system, subsystem, or process level so as to have the correct amount of contextual detail. Once done, the system purpose, outputs, and performance standards for that task can be specified and harmonized.

The systems flow results in a simplified diagram of the overall work system. Here the three major components of general systems theory — input, process, and output — are named. The core input, process, and output is called the *spine* of the system. Attached to the spine are the subsystems that more fully portray the complexity of the operating system. The systems spine is not a flowchart (see Chapter Thirteen or Zemke & Kramlinger, 1982). Once established, it is reasonable to produce a detailed flowchart of the spine once the system is conceptualized.

Systems Parts and Purposes

A more detailed understanding of the system is provided when identifying systems parts and purposes. This seemingly mundane step of analyzing systemic work is straightforward.

For example, do you call it the *hopper* or the *bin*? Talk to the employee who was told by his supervisor to clean out the bin (the size of a small house) when she really meant to clean out the hopper (the size of a desk) and he will tell you about the importance of terminology! Accurate terminology is an important outcome of all three types of task analysis. Tangible aspects of a system such as parts, data sets, documents, and the like should be named *and* their purpose described. The reality is that two workers in the same work system often don't see the same things, don't call them by the same name, and don't view them as having the same purpose. When this happens withiń systemic tasks, confusion can reign. For example, does *strategic plan* mean the same thing to each member of the senior management team?

Process Analysis

Process analysis helps to document the connections between the system and the various systems parts. In a perfectly logical system, the process variables (people, materials, equipment, method, and/or environment), their attributes, and their interconnections become apparent and display critical contributions to the effectiveness and efficiency of the system. As you might expect, process analysis also has the potential of identifying the disconnects, unwanted variation, overlaps, and unnecessary complexity that may have been designed into or grown into the system. The end result is a clearer picture of what changes are needed.

Troubleshooting Analysis

Based on the systems description, systems flow, systems parts and purposes, and process analysis, a network of the problems that *could* be encountered in the work system is specified. The troubleshooting options to these problems are organized into a troubleshooting analysis.

Checkpoint

Match the term on the right that best fits each of the following elements in systems task analysis.

___1. Systems description   a. *Spine*
___2. Systems flow   b. *Backward analysis*
___3. Systems parts and purposes   c. *Elements*
___4. Process analysis   d. *Forward analysis*
___5. Troubleshooting analysis   e. *Name*

Answers
1.e   2.a   3.c   4.d   5.b

Purchase Order System Case Study— The Voilà Company

The following is a systems analysis of the purchase order system within the Voilà Company. By way of an introduction, the output was determined to be an approval to purchase (Figure 12.2). The input is not a blank purchase order form, but rather an employee's need for materials or services. The purchase order process includes both conversion and transmission. Taking the determined need and recording it on a purchase order form is the *conversion*; forwarding the purchase order to an approval authority is the *transmission*.

Take the time now to review the organizational charts and the systems task analysis forms, letting them speak for themselves (Exhibit 12.1).

One variable for an acceptable purchase order system could be a request for quotations. The specification then could be: If an item costs $1,000 or more, it must go out for quotations. This specification could be displayed on the process analysis form.

Figure 12.2. Spine of the Voilà Purchase Order System.

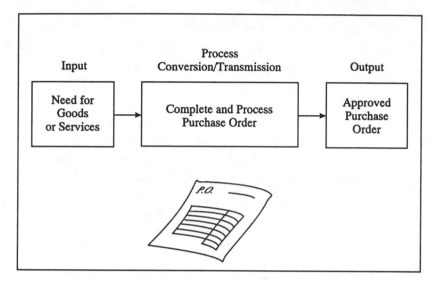

Within the existing process, the purchase cost variable requires quotations for purchases at or above $1,000. Any item costing more than $1,000 must be sent out for quotations. There is no special consequence for the plus deviation—that is, having a number of items valued at more than $1,000 on such a purchase order. However, any one item on a purchase order with a minus deviation—that is, having a value of less than $1,000—combined with other items over $1,000 would have process consequences. One consequence is the eight weeks required to complete the quotation process. Purchasing a single item of less than $1,000 takes only one day.

A second, *positive*, minus deviation consequence is a potentially lower purchase price resulting from sending items costing less than $1,000 out for quotation. The initial indicator is the estimated price from catalogs or from preliminary pricing per telephone request. The control is the person initiating the purchase order. Knowing the systemic conditions, specifications, indicators, controls, and effects of deviations is the key to process control and troubleshooting.

Exhibit 12.1. Voilà Company.

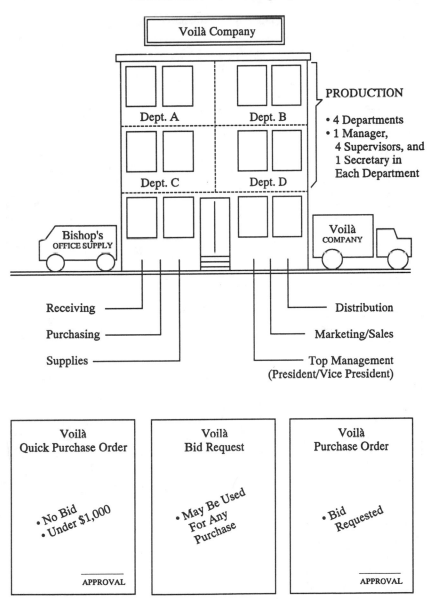

All Voilà Company salaried employees can initiate Purchase Orders.

Exhibit 12.1. Voilà Company, Cont'd.

Voilà Company Organizational Chart

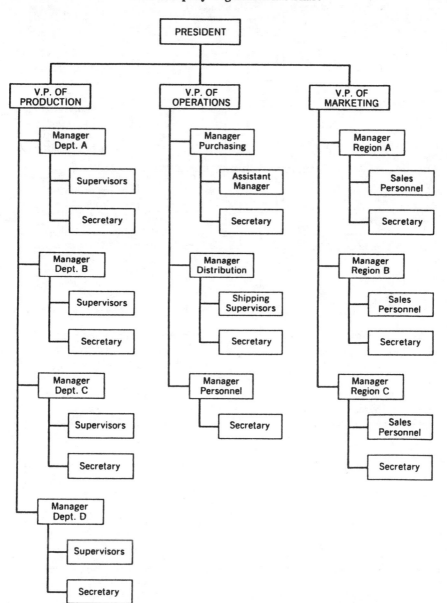

Exhibit 12.1. Voilà Company, Cont'd.

Systems Description and Flow

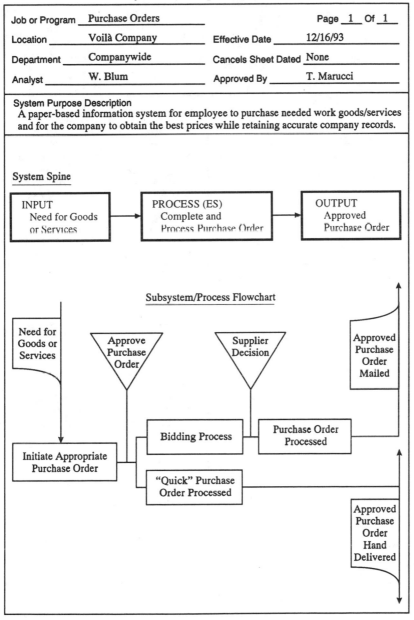

Exhibit 12.1. Voilà Company, Cont'd.

Systems Parts and Purposes

Job or Program Purchase Orders	Page 1 Of 1
Location Voilà Company	Effective Date 12/16/93
Department Companywide	Cancels Sheet Dated None
Analyst W. Blum	Approved By T. Marucci

PART Use Correct Nomenclature	PURPOSES Explain what the part does. Also explain how it works, if not obvious.
Voilà Purchase Order	– Company form that specifies the vendor, goods/services, conditions, and cost of a purchase. Must be used for all company purchases of $1,000 or more, and may be used for smaller purchases.
Voilà Quick Purchase Order	– Company form that specifies the vendor, goods/services, conditions, and cost of a purchase. Can be used for purchases under $1,000.
Voilà Bid Request	– Company form that requests a supplier's price for goods/services purchase.
Salaried Employees	– Company employees paid for services on an annual salary basis. Includes president, vice-presidents, managers, supervisors, and secretaries.
Purchasing Agent	– Salaried employee responsible for approving all purchases and initiating all purchase bids. Reports directly to the V.P. of Operations and Finance.

Exhibit 12.1. Voilà Company, Cont'd.

Process Analysis

Job or Program __Purchase Orders__

Location __Voilà Company__

Department __Companywide__

Analyst __W. Blum__

Page __1__ Of __1__

Effective Date __12/16/93__

Cancels Sheet Dated __None__

Approved By __T. Marucci__

VARIABLE	SPECIFICATION	INDICATOR	CONTROL	EFFECT OF		OTHER INFORMATION
				PLUS DEVIATION	MINUS DEVIATION	
Purchase Order over $1,000	Total cost of goods/services (including taxes) $1,000 or more	Figure on bottom line of purchase order	Purchasing Agent	Put out on bid	Reject Quick P.O.	
Purchase Order under $1,000	Total cost of goods/services (including taxes) less than $1,000	Figure on bottom line of purchase order	Purchasing Agent	Reject Quick P.O.	– 1 day to procure P.O. – Potential high cost to company for goods/services	
Bid or Not Bid under	Total cost of goods/services (including taxes) less than $1,000	Figure on bottom line of purchase order	Salaried employee requesting purchase	– Purchasing agent asks salaried employee if they want to bid – Potential lower costs to comapny	– 8 week process P.O. – Increased handling costs to company if put on bid	
Request for Bids	Total cost of goods/services (including taxes)	Over $1,000 or request from salaried employee	Purchasing Agent	Given estimated cost, send out on bid	If no estimated cost, no bid	

Exhibit 12.1. Voilà Company, Cont'd.

Troubleshooting Analysis

Job or Program	Purchase Orders		Page 1 Of 1
Location	Voilà Company	Effective Date	12/16/94
Department	Companywide	Cancels Sheet Dated	None
Analyst	W. Blum	Approved By	T. Marucci

PROBLEM	CAUSE	CORRECTIVE ACTION
Too long to get P.O. approval	– Using bid P.O. on items $1,000 or less	– Only use bid P.O. when required
	– Minimum of two bids not received in a timely fashion	– Increase the number of bid requests
Paying too high prices for goods	– Not obtaining bids on $1,000 or less items	– Put $1,000 items on a bid instead of "Quick P.O."
	– Not much range in bids received	– Increase number of bid requests

An item requiring a quotation takes eight weeks to purchase. In comparison, a nonquotation item takes one day to purchase. Work in an organization can stop because of a lack of supplies, and thus a nonresponsive purchasing system could create havoc with almost any operation. This circumstance can be averted if a nonquotation purchase order option is used instead of the quotation option. The one-day versus eight-week variation in purchase order processing is revealed to everyone through a process analysis. The one benefit of a potentially lower price with quotation is weighed against the shorter turnaround time. Troubleshooting analysis showed how this system would stop if the wrong purchase order procedure were used.

Systems Description and Flow: A Closer Look

As noted, naming the system or systemic work being analyzed is important. For example, the systems boundaries vary for the following names: *distribution, hiring truck drivers, fleet maintenance, dispatching*. The general description of the system to be studied, in the form of the systems purpose and the systems output, helps broker the analyst into specific systems performance standards.

In the systems flow step, the system and/or process is broken down into its components and the information or the materials from input to output are traced through the system. A systems flow diagram provides an understanding of the system and its elements—a view of the whole system from the required vantage point. Systems theory tells us that there are three basic components to any system: input(s), process(es), and output(s):

A systems flow grid worksheet (see the Appendix) and flow-chart symbols aid in graphically portraying the systems flow. Although most complex systems are made up of several sub-systems or processes, it is best to begin by defining the spine of the system under study. Usually it is preferable to first iden-tify the core output, then the core input(s), and finally the process(es).

You can isolate the spine by asking, "What is the major or core output of the system?" For example, the output of a delivery system is a product or service delivered to a specified destination at a specified time. To create a systems flow diagram, the analyst may either interview or accompany the delivery per-son to the final destination, noting the basic activities that take place prior and during final delivery, such as logging in with a dispatcher, signing off at the warehouse, recording data en route, carrying out the required activities at the customer site, sign-ing off for receipt of product or service, and so on. Each of these steps may then be expanded on, such as details of the en route recording of speed, mileage, fuel levels, and vehicle maintenance needs.

Let's take a simple, familiar hardware system—the incan-descent lightbulb—as an example. Given such a system, the first question to ask is, "What is the primary *output?*" In the case of the incandescent bulb, it is light. A second output of the incan-descent bulb is heat. In fact, you may have used heat lamps with bulbs specifically designed to produce heat, with light being the secondary, wasted output. In our example, the primary output is light.

What do you think the major *input* is? Some people might have written *coal.* Certainly, coal could be the source of energy at an electrical power production plant, but it is not the ready source of energy for the incandescent lightbulb system. Elec-tricity is the major input.

If you were analyzing an electrical power production sys-tem, coal could easily be an input. Because systems interact with other systems, and small systems can be nested within larger systems, *drawing boundaries around the system you are dealing with is crucial.* Otherwise, you will find yourself analyzing information that exceeds the knowledge required to perform the work, and by doing so, you will frustrate everybody. An appropriate system with its subsystems is defined by the performance demands on the worker and on the work system being analyzed.

The person who diagnoses and replaces failing or broken bulbs in building maintenance or in product research does not need to know about the larger power production system that includes coal as the input. Just knowing that electricity is the primary input to the incandescent lightbulb system is enough.

Now, what about the process in this incandescent light system? How is electricity transformed into light? The process stage of any system includes both transmission and conversion. In this case, the transmission is accomplished by the electron flow through wires, and the conversion is accomplished as a result of the resistance to the electrons flowing through a filament that heats up, glows, and gives off light — the output.

Checkpoint

Let's work through another example of systems flow, the automobile. In Figure 12.3, label the major elements that make up the

Figure 12.3. Systems Name: Automobile.

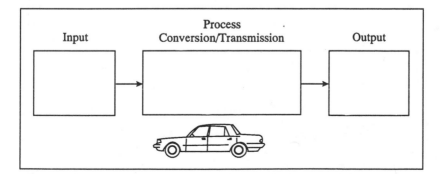

spine of the system. Remember to start with the output and then go to the input. Do the process last.

The automobile is a wonderful, familiar, and complex system. It has many subsystems, some of which have little or nothing to do with the intended output of motion. I identified fuel as the major input, with the conversion portion of the process being the engine and the transmission portion of the process being the drive train.

A stereo radio-cassette sound system as a subsystem of the automobile would be an absurd place to start figuring out the complex automobile system. The automobile does, however, have several subsystems that directly affect the major output of motion. One of these is the control system. The major controller of the automobile system is the driver. Add this to the spine of the automobile system (Figure 12.3) along with a cruise control subsystem. My version is shown in Figure 12.4.

The basic systems components of input, process, and output are useful in identifying the spine of a complex system. By

Figure 12.4. Driver and Cruise Control Subsystems.

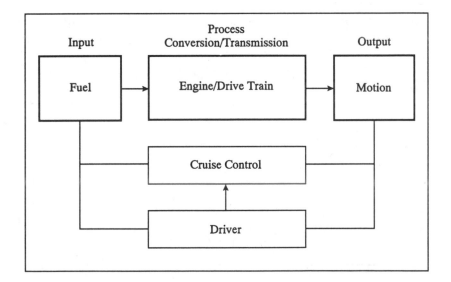

adding each of the subsystems, one can illustrate the complexity of the operation and the control components of the system. Familiarity with standard flowcharting symbols is useful but not mandatory. These symbols are shown in Figure 12.5. Using them allows the analyst to communicate in a standard and easily understood visual language.

Systems Parts and Purposes: A Closer Look

The product of a parts-and-purposes analysis is a summary list of the correct names and use(s) of the tangible parts of the system, including data with which people interact. This provides knowledge that will be used later in the troubleshooting analysis. A rule of thumb for creating a parts-and-purposes analysis is to include every systems element with which the worker interacts directly or indirectly. A list of systems parts and purposes for the employee benefits designer will differ from a list intended for the benefits claim processor. The designer will actually use items (such as tax law codes) of which the processor might only be aware. Obviously, there would be some overlapping of items on the two lists, but the claim processor's parts-and-purposes analysis might be longer (due to more numerous process steps), while the designer's would reflect a more conceptual process.

The systems parts-and-purposes form provides an accurate list of, and explanations for, all the process elements with which a worker interacts. Doing such an analysis for any system offers an excellent opportunity to name the systems parts correctly. The use of inconsistent terminology often causes confusion and frustration in the workplace among beginners and old-timers alike. For example, confusion results from references on the shop floor to a *fuel cap* one time, a *gas cap* another time, and a *tank cap* still another. The workplace is filled with inefficiencies resulting from miscommunication, often caused by the use of varying terminology. Here is your opportunity to straighten out some of the language in your workplace.

Figure 12.5. Systems Flow Symbols.

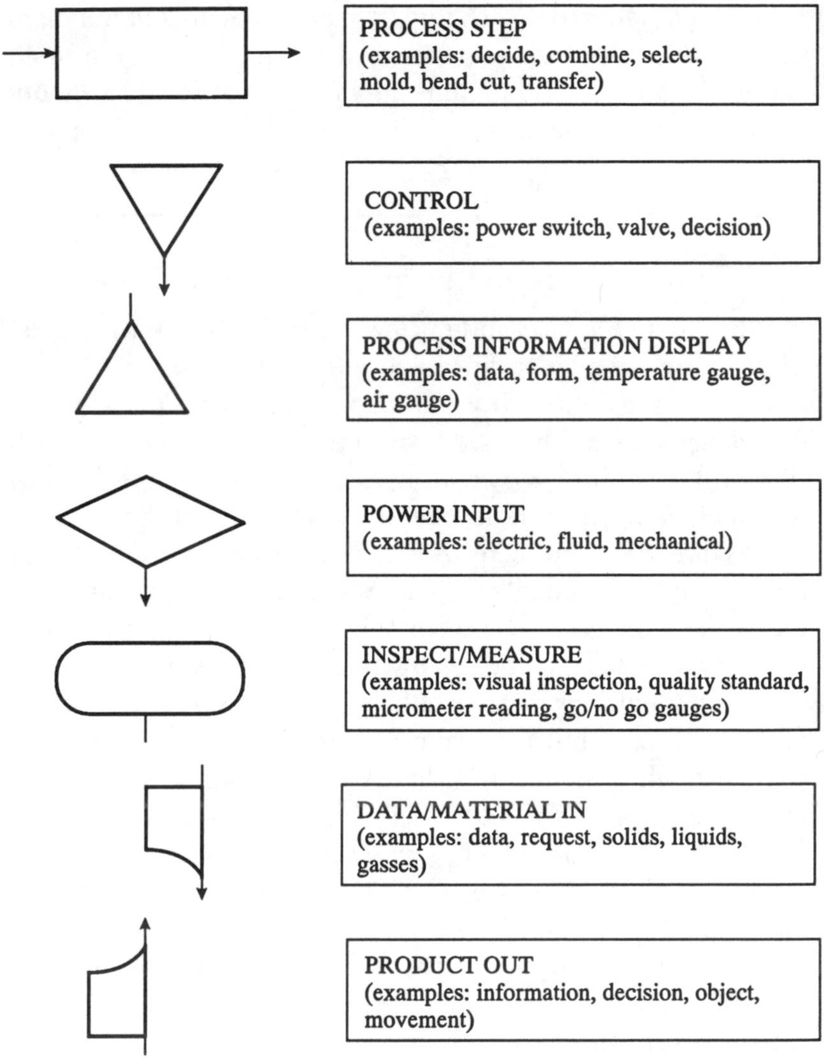

	PROCESS STEP (examples: decide, combine, select, mold, bend, cut, transfer)
	CONTROL (examples: power switch, valve, decision)
	PROCESS INFORMATION DISPLAY (examples: data, form, temperature gauge, air gauge)
	POWER INPUT (examples: electric, fluid, mechanical)
	INSPECT/MEASURE (examples: visual inspection, quality standard, micrometer reading, go/no go gauges)
	DATA/MATERIAL IN (examples: data, request, solids, liquids, gasses)
	PRODUCT OUT (examples: information, decision, object, movement)

Previously, we referred to subject experts as sources of knowledge. In analyzing systemic tasks, you will again want to use subject experts. In addition to relying on the subject experts in the organization, you will want to utilize expert knowledge from other sources, such as external consultants, original manufacturers of equipment, manuals, and technical information sheets.

Specialty books that provide detailed information are particularly helpful in preparing the systems flow diagram and conducting the parts-and-purpose analysis information and hardware systems. The authors may have already analyzed the process and explained the operation and handling of the components, thus saving you a great deal of time.

That old saying that knowledge is power begins to take on added meaning once a systems flow diagram and a systems parts-and-purposes analysis are completed. These two sets of information form the foundation for understanding systemic work tasks. So far, we have discussed the broad understanding that results from systems flow analysis and the essential knowledge that results from systems parts-and-purposes analysis. These two analyses are important but insufficient to provide the level of understanding needed to work with a complex system.

Process Analysis: A Closer Look

Process analysis is aimed at analyzing the system, or process, in operation. That is, you analyze how it works or functions. Process variables such as people, materials, equipment, method, and the process environment are identified in terms of their specifications, indicators, controls, and effects on the process Process variables are simply those human or hardware behaviors that change—for example, viscosity, temperature, timing, knowledge, decisions, satisfaction. Behind each possible variance is a metric such as yes or no, fifty degrees centigrade, or number in attendance. Actions that need to be performed regularly in *managing* the system, such as taking process measurement and communicating with suppliers for just-in-time delivery, are also identified by process analysis. This information is recorded on a process analysis form (see the Appendix).

Troubleshooting Analysis: A Closer Look

Troubleshooting analysis, the last step in the analysis of systemic tasks, yields the flow of diagnostic knowledge needed to respond to a sluggish, failing, or inoperative system. In this final component, you synthesize the systems flow, parts-and-purposes, and process analyses to complete your understanding of how to troubleshoot the system.

The troubleshooting analysis forms (see the Appendix) may appear to be more complex than they really are. The two earlier steps, systems flow and systems parts and purposes, prepare the analyst to move on to the troubleshooting analysis.

Remember that process analysis is forward looking and troubleshooting analysis is backward looking. Process analysis explains the operational theory of the system in a practical manner. Troubleshooting analysis takes the practical understanding of the fully operational system and applies it to a failed or failing system so the worker can get the system running. Even neglecting simple troubleshooting tasks can cause performance problems in the workplace, with the consequence being serious economic losses.

For any process, once potential problems have been identified along with their causes and corrective actions, they should be entered on the troubleshooting analysis form. How they are listed on the form will vary. Low-cost solutions should have priority. Low cost is calculated in terms of amount of worker time, systems downtime, and materials. Clearly, the desired solutions are those requiring as little of those three elements as possible. High-probability solutions have the next priority. High-probability solutions are apparent when a problem has only a few probable causes or when one solution to that problem has been successful in the past. Troubleshooting actions should therefore be listed in the following order:

1.   Low cost/high probability

2.   Low cost/low probability

3.   High cost/high probability

4.   High cost/low probability

The generally recommended order of troubleshooting is to focus first on low-cost and then on high-probability corrective actions. In fact, low-cost, low-probability corrective actions should be examined before high-probability, high-cost actions. For example, most of us have seen the home appliance troubleshooting charts that ask you first to check if your appliance is plugged in. The moment of time needed to investigate this low-cost, low-probability option could save many costly headaches. When we are confronted with a problem, most of us want to jump intuitively to the answer. The systems worker's knee-jerk reaction of knowing the answer can cause serious problems in the workplace. This is especially true when the costs of certain actions are high. The value of analyzing systemic work tasks should be clear by now.

Checkpoint: General Review

The following is a summary of the steps involved in analyzing systemic tasks. Answer the following questions; the answers provided should help you check your understanding of this analysis method.

From the example on the following page, match the correct definitions and examples on the right to the systems task analysis steps by placing the letters A, B, C, or D by the steps below.

Questions	Definition	Example
Step 1. Systems description and flow	_____	_____
Step 2. Systems parts and purposes	_____	_____
Step 3. Process analysis	_____	_____
Step 4. Troubleshooting analysis	_____	_____

Match Definitions and Examples to Steps

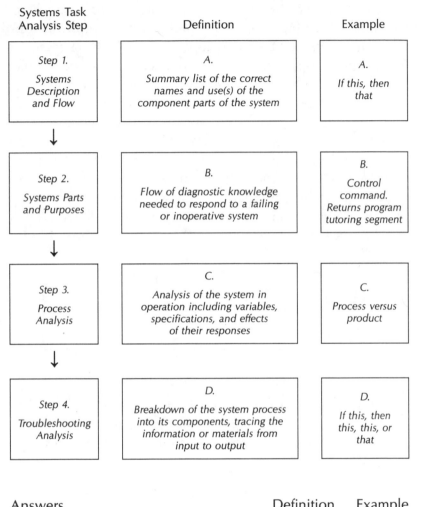

Systems Task Analysis Step	Definition	Example
Step 1. Systems Description and Flow	**A.** Summary list of the correct names and use(s) of the component parts of the system	**A.** If this, then that
Step 2. Systems Parts and Purposes	**B.** Flow of diagnostic knowledge needed to respond to a failing or inoperative system	**B.** Control command. Returns program tutoring segment
Step 3. Process Analysis	**C.** Analysis of the system in operation including variables, specifications, and effects of their responses	**C.** Process versus product
Step 4. Troubleshooting Analysis	**D.** Breakdown of the system process into its components, tracing the information or materials from input to output	**D.** If this, then this, this, or that

Answers	Definition	Example
Step 1. Systems description and flow	D	C
Step 2. Systems parts and purposes	A	B
Step 3. Process analysis	C	A
Step 4. Troubleshooting analysis	B	D

Checkpoint: Employee Assistance System Case Study

Study the analysis of the employee assistance system (Exhibit 12.2). Think about this system from the vantage point of two changes: (1) imagine that employee assistance benefits are extended to retirees for the first year following the date of retirement, and (2) imagine that employee assistance benefits are extended to employees in good standing who are terminated because of company restructuring (not poor performance) for up to two years following their date of termination or until they obtain employment. Answer the following questions in light of the two systems changes.

1. What changes would need to be made to the systems description and flow?

   a. Retirees _____

   _____

   b. Termination _____

   _____

2. What changes would need to be made to the systems parts and purposes?

   a. Retirees _____

   _____

   b. Termination _____

   _____

3. What changes would need to be made to the process analysis?

   a. Retirees _____

   _____

   b. Termination _____

   _____

4. What changes would need to be made to the troubleshooting analysis?

    a. *Retirees* _____

    _____

    b. *Termination* _____

    _____

Answers

1. *What changes would need to be made to the systems description and flow?*

    a. *Retirees* Add "for active employees and selected categories of retired and terminated employees."

    b. *Termination* _____

    _____

2. *What changes would need to be made to the systems parts and purposes?*

    a. *Retirees* Add two parts and their purposes: "Eligible retirees" and "Ineligible retirees."

    b. *Termination* Add two parts and their purposes: "Terminated, good standing" and "Terminated, poor standing."

3. *What changes would need to be made to the process analysis?*

    a. *Retirees* Add revised details to the "Eligible employee" and "Employee status" variables.

    b. *Termination* Add revised details to the "Eligible employee" and "Employee status" variables.

4. *What changes would need to be made to the troubleshooting analysis?*

    a. *Retirees* Add what constitutes an eligible retiree to the corrective action and cause columns.

    b. *Termination* Add what constitutes an eligible terminated employee to the corrective action and cause columns.

Exhibit 12.2. Employee Assistance System for ABC Company.

Systems Description and Flow

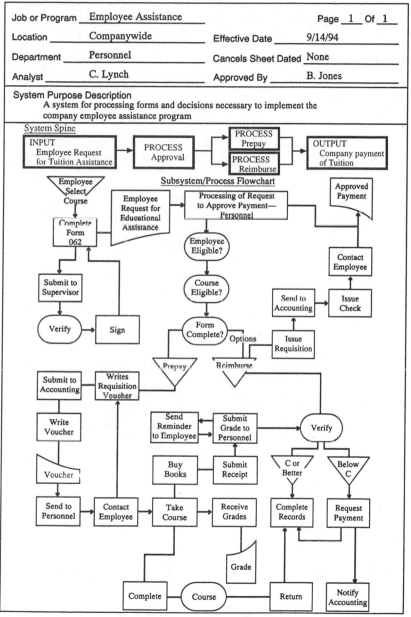

Job or Program	Employee Assistance		Page 1 Of 1
Location	Companywide	Effective Date	9/14/94
Department	Personnel	Cancels Sheet Dated	None
Analyst	C. Lynch	Approved By	B. Jones

System Purpose Description
A system for processing forms and decisions necessary to implement the company employee assistance program

System Spine

INPUT
Employee Request for Tuition Assistance → PROCESS Approval → PROCESS Prepay / PROCESS Reimburse → OUTPUT Company payment of Tuition

Subsystem/Process Flowchart

Employee Select Course

Complete Form 062

Employee Request for Educational Assistance

Processing of Request to Approve Payment— Personnel

Approved Payment

Submit to Supervisor

Employee Eligible?

Contact Employee

Verify — Sign

Course Eligible?

Send to Accounting — Issue Check

Form Complete? Options

Issue Requisition

Prepay / Reimburse

Submit to Accounting — Writes Requisition Voucher

Send Reminder to Employee — Submit Grade to Personnel — Verify

Write Voucher

Buy Books — Submit Receipt

C or Better / Below C

Voucher

Send to Personnel — Contact Employee — Take Course — Receive Grades — Complete Records — Request Payment

Grade

Complete — Course — Return — Notify Accounting

Exhibit 12.2. Employee Assistance System for ABC Company, Cont'd.

Systems Parts and Purposes

Job or Program __Employee Assistance__		Page __1__ Of __2__
Location __Companywide__	Effective Date __9/14/94__	
Department __Personnel__	Cancels Sheet Dated __None__	
Analyst __C. Lynch__	Approved By __B. Jones__	

PART Use Correct Nomenclature	PURPOSES Explain what the part does. Also explain how it works, if not obvious.
1. Eligible Employees	—All full-time active employees with at least satisfactory performance.
2. Eligible Courses	—Courses from accredited institutions that fill bank-related or general skill development needs and provide evidence of satisfactory completion.
3. Degree and Certificate Programs	—A planned course of study, approved by officer, that leads to a degree or certificate.
4. Tuition	—Required fees paid to the educational institution.
5. Reimbursement	—Payment paid to the employee/student on satisfactory completion of course for approved expenses of course.
6. Prepayment	—Payment to educational institution on behalf of employee/student before course is completed for approved expenses.
7. Satisfactory Grade Statement	—Notice that employee/student completed course at a satisfactory or better level, indicated by a Grade C or better, Pass, or signed statement from instructor on official letterhead.
8. Request for Educational Assistance Form	—Form 062-018 available from Personnel Department.
9. Independent Study	—Accredited course taken by correspondence or otherwise independent of classroom attendance.
10. Cash Voucher	—Form provided by Accounting Department that is redeemable for cash from the Special Services Window, Lobby.
11. Check	—Draft payment provided by Accounting Department that can be deposited or cashed.

Exhibit 12.2. Employee Assistance System for ABC Company, Cont'd.

Systems Parts and Purposes

Job or Program Employee Assistance	Page 2 Of 2
Location Companywide	Effective Date 9/14/94
Department Personnel	Cancels Sheet Dated None
Analyst C. Lynch	Approved By B. Jones

PART Use Correct Nomenclature	PURPOSES Explain what the part does. Also explain how it works, if not obvious.
12. Personnel Department	—Human Resources area, 2nd floor, administers educational assistance policy.
13. Accounting Department	—Expenses unit that issues payment.
14. Activity Code	—PACS number provided by employee's supervisor on Educational Assistance Request Form to designate the normal code number activity for that employee.
15. Nonreimbursable Fees	—Optional or non-course-related fees such as social, athletic, or late payment fees that are not absolutely required for the course.
16. Paylist	—Computer run providing information of employee status, tenure, performance, and disciplinary notice.

Exhibit 12.2. Employee Assistance System for ABC Company, Cont'd.

Process Analysis

Job or Program: Employee Assistance
Location: Companywide
Department: Personnel
Analyst: C. Lynch

Page 1 Of 2
Effective Date 9/14/94
Cancels Sheet Dated None
Approved By B. Jones

VARIABLE	SPECIFICATION	INDICATOR	CONTROL	EFFECT OF		OTHER INFORMATION
				PLUS DEVIATION	MINUS DEVIATION	
Courses selected	Bank-related content; limit of 2 per term	Organization Dir. description of duties	Review by Personnel	Limit of 2 or policy exception	1 is OK	Non-bank-related can be approved under Degree program
Amount requested	Actual cost up to U-M rate; books limited to $35	Univ. Bulletin	Review by Personnel	Reduce request to limit	Tax-deduction	If unable to take lower-cost course because of work-required travel, exception is made
Eligible employee	Full time; satisfactory performance	Info on form	Paylist	Supervisor may not approve	Ineligible	Exception if needed for job improvement or required by supervisor
Form of payment	Reimbursement: any eligible employee	Checked on form	Personnel req.	None	None	
Form of payment	Prepayment; 3 months tenure	Checked on form	Paylist	None	Ineligible	Also ineligible if more than 4 requests are still outstanding

Exhibit 12.2. Employee Assistance System for ABC Company, Cont'd.

Process Analysis

Job or Program Employee Assistance

Location Companywide

Department Personnel

Analyst C. Lynch

Effective Date 9/14/94

Cancels Sheet Dated None

Approved By B. Jones

VARIABLE	SPECIFICATION	INDICATOR	CONTROL	EFFECT OF		OTHER INFORMATION
				PLUS DEVIATION	MINUS DEVIATION	
Books needed	$35/course	Syllabus	Receipts	Employee pays	Actual cost	
Course term	Quarter or semester	Catalog description	Standard	Limit within standard	None	Occurs with vocational school programs
Time to issue check	Allow 5 days	Application form	Personnel Admin.	30 days	24 hours	Contact acct.
Grade	C or better	Transcript	Review by Personnel	OK	No pay	Must repay if prepaid
Employee status	Active	Paylist	Review by Personnel	OK	No pay	Must repay if prepaid

Exhibit 12.2. Employee Assistance System for ABC Company, Cont'd.

Troubleshooting Analysis

Job or Program	Employee Assistance		Page 1 Of 2
Location	Companywide	Effective Date	9/14/94
Department	Personnel	Cancels Sheet Dated	None
Analyst	C. Lynch	Approved By	B. Jones

PROBLEM	CAUSE	CORRECTIVE ACTION
Ineligible application	– Incomplete information	– Call employee to obtain information
Ineligible employee	– Unsatisfactory performance	– Contact supervisor for exemption for cause, or reject application
	– Written notice	– Reject application
	– More than 2 requests	– Reject request
Employee status change	– Employee leave or termination	– Write employee and present payment plan and tax benefits
	– Change to hourly	– Notify employee of ineligibility and payment plan options or consider deferring start of hourly employment
Ineligible course	– Not bank-related	– Reject application unless part of degree program and recommend degree program to employee if appropriate
Tuition excessive	– Course at nonpublic institution	– Recommend public course or reduce cost allowable and notify employee
Application withdrawn	– Course full or canceled	– Remove application from active file and note reason; call back payment
Employee new to bank (ineligible for prepayment)	– New hire	– Provide reimbursement
Employee lacks tuition money	– Low income/other expenses	– Prepayment option: Bank pays initial cost, contingent on satisfactory course completion
Grades not in	– Employee drops or fails course	– Require repayment if prepaid
		– File request in canceled file and correct record if reimbursement had been requested
	– Employee takes an incomplete	– Request memo asking extension and extend period 60 days
	– Institution loses grade	– Request documentation on official letterhead from instructor

Exhibit 12.2. Employee Assistance System for ABC Company, Cont'd.

Troubleshooting Analysis

Job or Program __Employee Assistance__		Page _2_ Of _2_
Location __Companywide__	Effective Date _____9/14/94_____	
Department __Personnel__	Cancels Sheet Dated _None_	
Analyst __C. Lynch__	Approved By _____B. Jones_____	

PROBLEM	CAUSE	CORRECTIVE ACTION
Employee status change	– Termination	– Contact payroll before final pay issued and request employee to authorize payroll deduction; if final pay issued, write employee and request repayment
	– Unsatisfactory performance	– Contact payroll and employee, as above
	– Change to hourly	– Same as above

Acme, Inc. — Analyzing the
Systems Task of Monitoring and
Troubleshooting Shipping Operations

The Acme, Inc. case study in Chapter Three offered an overview of an organization with performance problems. Chapter Six featured a performance improvement proposal for the Acme Shipping Department. The proposal included the recommendation to strengthen the job of shipper, partly by training all the job incumbents. The description of the job of shipper was included in Chapter Nine, and the task inventory for this job was found in Chapter Ten. One of the seven tasks on the inventory was "Process seat cover order" (Task 2); it was analyzed in Chapter Eleven. Task 4, "Monitor and troubleshoot shipping operations," is a systemic task. Exhibit 12.3 provides the analysis of that task.

Tips for the Analyst

Systems work analysis focuses on tasks of information-based systems and hardware systems and is used to describe complex work behaviors under abnormal conditions. Like other analysis methods, analysis of systems tasks provides its share of revelations. In systems tasks, what appears to be obvious often ends up not being true. This is why systems task analysis is needed.

The subtleties of working with systems generally prove to be difficult for both the worker and the analyst. The ultimate goal of the systems task analysis is to improve the system or enhance employee expertise so that workers will no longer be unsure of their role within the system. Following a full systems task analysis, what initially appeared to be a confusing and complex set of work behavior issues can become a simple set of procedural statements or a detailed process flowchart.

Having to operate both within a system and under abnormal conditions adds dimensions to any job. These dimensions need to appear on the original job description and task inventory. Systems task analysis does not always result in adding more tasks to the task inventory form, however. In fact, the opposite can at times be true.

Exhibit 12.3. Analysis of Shipper's Systems Task.

Systems Description and Flow

Job or Program	#4-Monitor and Troubleshoot Shipping Operations Page 1 Of 1
Location	St. Paul, Minn. Effective Date 1/1/95
Department	Shipping Cancels Sheet Dated None
Analyst	R. Torraco Approved By Dept. Head

Systems Purpose/Description:
The shipping system processes customer orders for ACME seat covers. It involves customer requests for specific items that shippers select, pack, and ship.

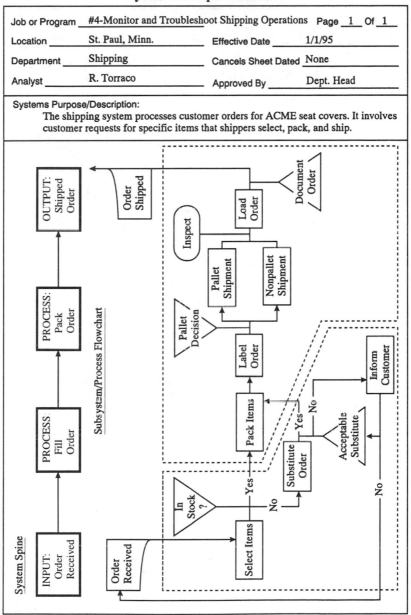

Exhibit 12.3. Analysis of Shipper's Systems Task, Cont'd.

Systems Parts and Purposes

Job or Program __Shipper__	Page _1_ Of _1_
Location _____St. Paul, Minn._____	Effective Date _____1/1/95_____
Task #4-Monitor and Troubleshoot Shipping Operations	Cancels Sheet Dated None
Department _____Shipping_____	Approved By _____Dept. Head_____
Analyst _____R. Torraco_____	

PART Use Correct Nomenclature	PURPOSES Explain what the part does. Also explain how it works, if not obvious.
Seat Covers	The primary product manufactured and distributed by ACME. Referred to as *parts,* there are over 130 different seat covers offered for sale.
Order Ticket	The document generated by the Order Handling Department in response to customer requests for products that specifies all the data necessary to process and invoice a seat cover order.
Parts Bin	Large containers within which seat covers of the same part number are stored in inventory. Each part number has its own parts bin.
Shipping Container	Reusable, reinforced cardboard containers in which parts are shipped to customer.
Conveyor Belt	An automated system linking all levels and sectors of the warehouse used for the internal transport of shipping containers. Conveyor belt movement is manually started and stoped by the shipper.
Flatbed Cart	A manually loaded, four-wheeled vehicle used by the shipper to internally transport shipping containers within the warehouse.
Shipping Pallet	A portable, wooden platform for storing, moving, and shipping ACME products.
Shipping Mode	The method of shipment used to transport ACME products to customers. There are three shipment modes: *ground transport, air transport,* and *international air.* The mode of shipment is determined by the customer's distance from the ACME distribution point.
Delivery Carrier	The transportation company used to transport ACME product to customers. In addition to ACME, approved delivery carriers include UPS, DHL, and U.S. Express.
Distribution Director	Person responsible for the policies and direction of the distribution function in ACME.
Shipping Supervisor	Person responsible for overseeing total shipping process.
Shipper	Person responsible for processing customer orders.
Shipping Clerk	Person responsible for maintaining shipping department records.
Customer	Person and/or organization ordering seat covers.

Exhibit 12.3. Analysis of Shipper's Systems Task, Cont'd.

Process Analysis

Job or Program __Shipper__

Location __St. Paul, Minn.__

Task __#4-Monitor and Troubleshoot Shipping Operations__

Department __Shipping__

Analyst __R. Torraco__

Effective Date __1/1/95__   Page __1__ Of __1__

Cancels Sheet Dated __None__

Approved By _____ Dept. Head

VARIABLE	SPECIFICATION	INDICATOR	CONTROL	EFFECT OF		OTHER INFORMATION
				PLUS DEVIATION	MINUS DEVIATION	
Inventory status of part(s)	In stock or Out of stock	Computerized display of inventory status	Level of production of part(s), and	Excess parts in inventory	No parts in inventory	
		Presence of part(s) on warehouse shelf	Level of customer demand for part(s)			
Customer acceptance of substituted parts	Approval or disapproval of substitution	Communication with customer	Substitute parts or expedite production of parts originally ordered	N/A	Terminate processing of substituted parts	
Speed of shipment delivery	*Priority* shipment is delivered within 24 hours of order	Speed shipment selected by customer (see *Delivery Speed* indicated on order)	Shipper selects proper mode of shipment to meet specified delivery time	N/A	Parts delivered late	
	Standard shipment is delivered within 2–3 days of order					

Exhibit 12.3. Analysis of Shipper's Systems Task, Cont'd.

Troubleshooting Analysis

Job or Program __Shipper__		Page _1_ Of _1_
Location ____St. Paul, Minn.____	Effective Date ____1/1/95____	
Task _#4-Monitor and Troubleshoot Shipping Operations_	Cancels Sheet Dated _None_	
Department ____Shipping____	Approved By ____Dept. Head____	
Analyst ____R. Torraco____		

Performance Standard:
Shippers will be the first to recognize and report operations that are failing and be proactive members of operations troubleshooting teams. The result will be increased up-time, order fulfillment, and fewer returns.

PROBLEM	CAUSE	CORRECTIVE ACTION
Parts not in stock.	Production of parts inadequate to meet demand.	Increase production of out-of-stock parts.
	Parts misplaced in inventory.	Ensure that parts are properly stored according to ACME inventory system.
Incorrect parts information on Order Ticket.	Order Ticket improperly coded.	Ensure that requests for parts are confirmed with customer and coded with correct ACME part number.
Incomplete parts information on Order Ticket.	Parts information not obtained or coded by Order Handling Department.	Ensure that requests for parts are confirmed with customer. Complete *Order Ticket* with all information necessary for processing order.
Incorrect customer information on Order Ticket.	Change of address of current customer.	Confirm customer name, account number, and address with each order.
	Customer account does not match customer.	Confirm customer name, account number, and address with each order.
	Incomplete customer information on file.	Do not initiate order processing without *Customer Status Approval* from ACME Sales office.
Delay in shipment departure.	Proper *Shipment Mode* unavailable.	Contract for delivery through an alternate mode of shipment.
	Parts for complete order unavailable.	Fill order with originally specified or substituted parts.
Delay of shipment en route.	Mechanical breakdown.	Ensure delivery carriers meet shipping contract obligations.
	Order shipped to incorrect address.	Ensure correct customer information on *Order Ticket.*

Conclusion

The process of analyzing systems tasks has introduced you to a set of unique documentation tools — systems description and flow, systems parts and purposes, process analysis, and troubleshooting analysis.

While the tools have been used here to detail what a person needs to know and be able to do to perform part of a job — a systems task — the method can be applied to any systemic level. Thus, these tools also have great utility for analyzing the process performance level of organizational diagnosis (Chapter Five). How about a systems analysis of the global market or the industry in which your company operates? The company in which your department operates? The process that links workers to workers and workers to customers? Systems analysis can help develop a more accurate picture and understanding of the selected system, the connections among subsystems, and the expertise required of those connections and handoffs from one expert worker to another.

The next chapter describes the process of analyzing knowledge tasks, a method for documenting knowledge work — or people-idea and people-people work behavior. This third tool will complete your toolbox for analyzing job tasks.

Chapter 13

Knowledge
Task Analysis

Thus far we have described work behaviors that have been visible, or nearly so. The analyst has been able to follow the logic of these work behaviors by observing and questioning workers about step-by-step procedures or by studying the various systems with which employees work. But not all work behaviors are overtly observable, and not every worker knows exactly how, when, or why certain work behaviors are more effective than others.

Coaching workers, analyzing equipment requirements, planning projects, handling grievances: these are complex work tasks in which the individuals doing the work define most of the work behavior. Although some work behaviors may be observed (for example, we may see people scratching their heads as they think), and the results of work behaviors may be observed (subordinates walking away angry or satisfied; projects failing or succeeding), most of the work of thinking, analyzing, and deciding is not visible. The *knowledge task analysis* method addresses such nonvisible work behaviors — people-idea and people-people workplace expertise.

Why the requirement to analyze such abstract, ill-defined work behaviors? Before answering this question, let's ask a few more: Are certain salespeople, decision makers, supervisors, and investors better at what they do than others who perform similar tasks? What are the differences between the expert and the not-so-expert performers? Would knowing these differences be beneficial in hiring, coaching, and promoting people; in job design or organizational design; and in research and strategic planning? You bet it would!

The following incident is an example of what can happen as the result of superficial task analyses.

MEMORANDUM
TO: All Department Heads
FROM: The Boss
SUBJECT: Training

I am pleased to announce that Mr. Consultant will be presenting a workshop on Handling Turnover Problems. We will meet at the Holly Hotel on the 20th. As previously agreed, your department may send one representative. Send in the name of your representative by the 15th!

Manager: "Hey Hank. Look at this memo. The boss is spending big bucks on having another trainer come to town. Who should we send this time?"

Supervisor: "Joe has been keeping his nose to the grindstone lately. Let him go if he wants to. Or you could send Jane. She likes to get out and meet people. She thinks it's good for her career."

Question: What work performance is lacking in this department that will be improved by Joe's or Jane's attending this workshop?

Answer: We don't know, and the manager doesn't know either.

Many managers are beginning to recognize the limitations of short-term, short-sighted organizational development, management development, and employee training. Knowledge task analysis gives us the tools to identify these critical knowledge work behaviors, the ones that have the potential of affecting performance on the job and thus productivity.

Process of Analyzing Knowledge Tasks

First, let's review the steps in analyzing a knowledge task, as shown in Figure 13.1.

Figure 13.1. Analyzing Knowledge Tasks.

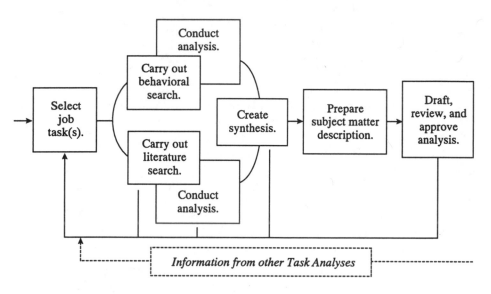

You begin, in step one, to investigate a subject or area of expertise that was derived through a performance diagnosis and specified as a task on a task inventory. Your subject matter is not procedural, nor does it involve a regularly performed systems work task. Your subject is an area of knowledge which, if mastered, would contribute to or enhance work behaviors. In one job, a knowledge of the chemistry of paints would improve performance. In another job, knowing the latest technology in composite materials is a requirement. In still another job, a knowledge of group process or decision making in business might be particularly useful. Any subject is a candidate for analysis as long as success in the workplace hinges on the workers' knowing the subject.

Having identified the knowledge task from the performance improvement proposal and task inventory, you proceed with the investigation along two paths: (1) the collection and analysis of behavior in the workplace; (2) the collection and analysis of literature by theorists, researchers, and other experts on the subject. Pursuing the investigation through a behavioral search alone will give you a biased and incomplete view of the subject matter—you will be able to describe practices and constraints but will gain little understanding of the scope of the subject or of the many available alternatives. Pursuing the investigation through a literature search alone will leave the realities of the workplace out of your analysis.

In the workplace, as part of the behavioral search, you can study effective and ineffective work behaviors so as to gain insight into the critical theories, methods, or technical knowledge connected to successful job performance. By interviewing people and presenting questionnaires, by observing the work environment and the results of particular work behaviors, and by reviewing performance records, you assess the knowledge, skills, and attitudinal components of job expertise. Your goal is a complete picture of the performance area under investigation.

In the alternative path of investigation, the literature search, you search for and collect printed materials on the subject. Reference manuals, multijournal indexes, computer searches, bibliographies—these are your tools when searching for specific information in the literature.

You may pursue the two paths of investigation, behavioral search and literature search, either concurrently or consecutively. You examine and analyze the behavioral data collected and all the reference notes from the literature search for completeness and relevance. I have found that it is critical to put the key

points of each source in your own words, not the words of the
author. Next, you perform a synthesis of all the data collected.
Using one or more of eight knowledge synthesis tools to be
described later in this chapter, you organize, combine, and conceptualize the data into a simplified knowledge or performance
model that shows the relationships among the detailed aspects
of the subject matter.

The final step in the knowledge task analysis method is to
produce a well-organized written description of information
about the subject that captures the workplace expertise of the
skilled performer. The subject matter description may be in the
form of either a narrative or a detailed outline. It should contain all the subject matter content needed to perform properly
at work, plus a list of the analyst's primary information sources.

Let's look at how one analyst planned to conduct a knowledge work analysis.

Planning a Knowledge Task Analysis

Marilyn Theobolt, director of Personnel Services, is given a particularly difficult assignment. James Martinez, vice president of
Human Resources at Reese Manufacturing, has informed her
that three women have complained about being harassed at
Reese and that this is at least two incidents too many. Martinez wants to know the legal definition of sexual harassment,
whether it is a problem for women in the company, and what
other companies are doing about the problem. Fortunately, Theobolt is well qualified to handle the assignment. Because she
has completed several such analyses in the past, she is familiar
with the process of working through all the steps. This time,
though, she decides to work a bit smarter; she will plan the
project first. The following is her plan of action, which she may
change or add to as she continues with her analysis.

PLAN FOR ANALYZING A KNOWLEDGE TASK

Job: All Management Personnel, Reese, Inc.
Date: (month/day/year)
Analyst: M. Theobolt

Task or Subject Matter:
Defining Sexual Harassment and Managing Sexual Harassment Grievances

Behavioral Search (Methods and Sources):
Interview J. Martinez, review complaint records, consult with a lawyer, and distribute an anonymous response questionnaire to a sample of women employees.

Behavioral Analysis Methods:
Analyze who, what, when, where, how, and why employees are seemingly being ill-treated at Reese. Who is not and seemingly why?

Literature Search (Methods and Sources):
Read articles in files, locate other references, and call federal office for regulations.

Literature Analysis Methods:
Create a database of important facts (computer and/or cards); incorporate historical legal, cultural, and economic aspects, including definitions. Who is harassed? Why?

Synthesis Model(s):
Select and use at least two of the methods. One for understanding the elements? One for process information?

Subject Matter Description (Format and Features):
Write up the details of sexual harassment in outline form for defining and understanding sexual harassment in the workplace. Include full citations of all important data sources.

Task or Subject Matter Identification

This step is easy. Theobolt and Martinez have already conducted a performance diagnosis. The final performance proposal established the performance requirement of (1) company compliance with sexual harassment laws and (2) managers being able to follow sexual harassment grievance process. The first performance issue required a company policy, process, and communication at the understanding level to all employees. The second performance issue resulted in a new task for all managers in the company and the required expertise in implementing the process.

Behavioral Search

For this step, Theobolt knows she can interview people, observe people at work, distribute questionnaires, and search company records. She decides to do everything but observe people at work. She figures that the behavior she is studying will not be done openly. Because interviewing is time consuming, she will limit interviewing to only a few persons. Other methods she could include in her plan are: talking to many people, watching people at work, conducting a group interview, and so forth.

Behavioral Analysis

Theobolt knows from experience that this step often involves pulling her information together to see where the holes are and where else she needs to look. Other methods she can include in her plan are: tossing out the extraneous data, sorting the information into useful categories, checking the information gathered from one group of people against that gathered from their supervisors, looking for contradictions, and the like.

Literature Search

In Theobolt's file drawer are copies of articles from the *Human Resource Management* and *Human Resource Development Quarterly* publications on the topic of sexual harassment. She keeps extensive files on current topics and is known for being able to come up with articles when others need them. When her needs go beyond her personal resources, she uses the services of the public library. She could also decide to review the reference list at the end of the article, ask the librarian to make a computer search for appropriate articles, or call the local U.S. government information office, among other alternatives.

Literature Analysis

Years of experience have taught Theobolt to keep reference notes on cards. Cards can be grouped, sequenced, or cut many different ways to reveal patterns of information. She will write the ideas on the cards in her own words. This forces her to analyze the material as she reads it. She pays attention to who was quoted most often and to the material that shows up on many reference lists.

Synthesis and Subject Matter Description

This part of her plan will be finalized when she is further along in her search. In a folder on her desk, she keeps a variety of paper forms that will help her in her synthesis and subject matter description steps.

Such plans have a way of changing as the analyst proceeds through the task. Nevertheless, creating a plan is a critical first step. Theobolt visualizes carrying out her plan while she does her behavioral and literature searches. She will change her plan as she discovers new possibilities for analyzing the subject matter assigned to her.

Checkpoint

In Chapters Nine and Ten, you wrote your own job description and created a task inventory. If any of the tasks requires you to interact with people or manipulate ideas or understand an unclear system in your organization, such a task probably qualifies as an area of work behavior suitable for a knowledge task analysis. You may want to take a few minutes at this time to develop a plan to analyze one of the knowledge tasks on your task inventory.

Taking the Behavioral Search and Analysis Paths

Analysts who want firsthand information about people and performance must make a behavioral search. They must go into the world of work to get accurate information. The task of search-

ing and analyzing information on work behavior in an organizational setting is a demanding one, but it can be as much fun
as reading a good mystery. In analyzing knowledge tasks, the
four most commonly used behavioral search techniques are interviews, questionnaires, observations, and organizational records. Each technique has its appropriate uses, and each demands
competence in searching for and analyzing information. These
are the same four data collection techniques used in diagnosing workplace performance and that were covered in depth in
Chapter Seven.

Taking the Literature Search
and Analysis Path

No analyst worth his or her salt would drop a knowledge task
analysis after gathering behavioral data. It is equally important
for you to learn what other theorists and expert practitioners
have thought about or done in such performance situations.
What behaviors, concepts, models, and rules have people found
to be effective or ineffective in similar circumstances? What
criteria and measuring rods have other experts used? What are
some feasible alternatives? It is time for you to begin to search
the literature on the subject you are investigating.

Case of the Manager Under Pressure

Ken Morris was notified that he must improve productivity in the
Hardware Division by 10 percent next year. Just last month he
had accepted, on behalf of his employees, the best-division award
for overall improvement of operations. But, with their competitors giving them a run for their money, the division must improve still more. At a special meeting that afternoon, one of his
staff members said she had just heard her friend in another part
of the company rave about a brilliant consultant who espoused
situational leadership as a method for improving productivity.

     She volunteered to make a literature search of the subject.
She contacted the company librarian first. He asked a few questions and established some concepts and keywords for the infor-

mation she wanted. Then he sat down at his computer terminal and called up a business management database. First he entered the keyword *productivity* and learned that in the database, there were 4,000 entries from books and U.S. and foreign journals that mentioned the word *productivity* in the title or in an abstract of the work. He entered the term *leadership* next and found nearly 1,400 entries. He combined the two terms and queried the database again. Fewer than 70 entries mentioned productivity and leadership together. Aha! This was becoming a more manageable project. Finally, he asked for entries that combined the terms *productivity* and *leadership* added either *situation* or *situational* as a modifier. Beyond the search printout, the librarian thought a manual search should be made. He recommended that the staff member go to the public library and ask the librarian there to guide her through a search of print indexes.

At the public library, she consulted the *Business Periodicals Index*. Explored might be a better word. Under *productivity*, she discovered references to articles titled "Managing Productivity in Organizations," "Productivity Planning and Measuring the Results," "Productivity Myths," and "After the Grid and Situationalism: A Systems View." Under leadership she found articles titled "Leadership Style Training: A Myth," "Situational Leadership Theory: A Review," and "The Myth of Leadership Style Training and Planning Organizational Change." She expected to find several relevant articles among these. Perhaps she would find information that corroborated the consultant's claim. Either way, it promised to be an interesting search.

Using a Keyword Search

Efficiency in a literature search in this age of computer-based indexes depends on narrowing your subject matter to a few key words, just as the librarian did in the preceding example. The search began by asking for a count of citations containing the term *productivity* or *leadership*, then *productivity* and *leadership*, then *productivity* with *situational* as the modifier for *leadership*. In the last instance, the search located only one citation.

In this case, the analyst may have specified the subject too narrowly. One article, one book, or one chapter will rarely present a diversity of opinions or ideas on a subject. The analyst must search the print indexes next.

Using the Print Indexes

The following are some of the indexes and resources available in most large public or university libraries: card catalog or microfiche, *Reader's Guide to Periodical Literature, Business Periodicals Index* (an index of 200 business-oriented journals), articles index for the *Wall Street Journal* or the *New York Times, Social Science Index* (2,000 journals), and *Work in America Studies.*

Such print indexes are frequently used for finding materials about business subjects. They lag three months or more behind the actual publication dates of the materials they list and thus are not quite as up to date as computer-based indexes. Nevertheless, you will find that print indexes are current enough for most of your research needs. The fact that you can more easily locate materials closely related to your topic in print indexes than in computer-based indexes is a benefit not to be undervalued or ignored. In print indexes, too, you will find many side streets and alleys to explore in search of materials on your subject.

Should you make a computer search or a search of print indexes? The decision is yours, but I recommend that you consider doing both.

Often overlooked by the new analyst are some fine opportunities to take advantage of the work done by previous researchers. Annotated bibliographies and references cited at the end of scholarly articles offer a wealth of resources. Reference manuals and professional handbooks will help to pinpoint the topic within the larger context in which it figures importantly — a big-picture view that an analyst sometimes ignores when pursuing detailed information about a subject.

Now aren't you curious about what you will find when you do an actual computer search on your chosen subject? Ask your librarian to make such a search for you — especially if your subject is currently being discussed in the print media. The cost to you is minimal, covering the long distance telephone call and the computer search time.

Perhaps you are curious about the results of an exploratory trip through the print indexes. This activity requires that you invest more time than money, but I assure you that you will be richly rewarded.

Analysis

Twelve articles, four books, one video training tape, and two monographs—how does anyone begin to analyze this much detailed material? Perhaps you already have your own method for absorbing and classifying print information.

The following method is recommended: First, review each resource for its relevance to your subject, its timeliness, and the accuracy and usefulness of the ideas it contains. Discard any resource that does not fit your needs. If you need more material, go back to the indexes and search again. Second, read the materials you have gathered and think about what you have read. What useful or important ideas, approaches, or findings did the material contain? Third, write notes about what you have read *in your own words*. On copies of articles, write the important ideas in the margins. Argue with the author. Ask questions and look for the answers.

Skilled analysts have learned that merely highlighting the text or copying the author's words on note cards—or any other method of parroting information—does not facilitate analysis. Such tactics only add clutter and confusion to the work of analysis. The exception to this rule, of course, is your need to collect particularly relevant quotations. These you will copy into a computer-based bibliographic reference system.

At the end of your literature search, you will have a collection of important ideas, a historical perspective or context for the subject matter, an awareness of what is relevant and what is not, and some notion of how the information may be applied effectively to accomplish the job task.

A thorough behavioral search and analysis plus an equally thorough literature search and analysis will yield great quantities of material on cards, papers, and computer disks and in the memory of the analyst. What can be done with such a collection of detail to make it useful? The step of combining the results of the behavioral search with the results of the literature search is next.

Synthesizing the Data

Analysis is taking apart and examining pieces of collected data. *Synthesis* is pulling the pieces together again and simplifying and organizing them in a meaningful way. Synthesis is an essential step in analyzing the subject matter of knowledge tasks. Just as a kite cannot be flown as a collection of pieces — tail, string, frame, and fabric — so subject matter cannot be used when it is in the form of a collection of bits of information. It is up to you, the analyst, to integrate and shape the detailed facts and impressions you have collected into usable, meaningful wholes.

Some analysts do this synthesis step easily, almost unconsciously. Others find themselves juggling vast quantities of unrelated data, which either remain up in the air or come crashing down in messy heaps. Eventually, these amateur analysts simply choose to select a few manageable pieces of the data and discard the rest. Such arbitrary choosing inevitably results in their leaving out crucial information. The goal, then, is to include in a synthesis all of the material that is important and useful. This is not a simple step, but expert synthesizing can be learned.

Expert synthesizers were studied to determine how they approach their tasks of turning collections of information into meaningful wholes (Swanson, 1981). Despite the fact that they had trouble describing their mental processes precisely, these experts asserted that they always begin to synthesize with a rich store of information. They gather their data, they analyze it, and then they work with it. Then, using systematic patterns of thinking, they combine, argue with, select, compose, relate, summarize, organize, conceptualize, simplify, arrange, and fit the information into a synthesis. They find a synthesis that is logical, encompasses the data, and holds meaning for themselves and others. Some prefer using a single favorite synthesis technique; others use a variety of techniques.

Abraham Maslow probably did not set out to create his famous *hierarchy of needs*. He studied people and thought about them and their motivations. The notions of levels of need and of decreasing instances of need fit his data well. Voilà, a hierarchy! Such a synthesis process is not magical. Synthesis models are created by disciplined minds.

What Is a Synthesis Model?

A synthesis model is a structure, in words or on paper, that is used to organize and communicate a large amount of information — facts, ideas, impressions, attitudes, or opinions — about a subject. The synthesis may be one-, two-, or three-dimensional. Because you are reading this book, I assume that you read business-oriented publications and participate in business training seminars. Undoubtedly, you regularly encounter synthesis models. Herzberg's theory X and theory Y styles of management and Covey's seven habits of highly effective people are synthesis models. With their models these authors have provided us with unique frameworks within which to simplify, organize, and portray great quantities of information about the subject of management.

But one model will not fit all situations. You will benefit from having a variety of models at hand.

Eight Types of Synthesis Models

Our expert synthesizers described eight synthesis techniques:

- Reflection
- Two-axis matrix
- Three-axis matrix
- Flowchart
- Events network

- Dichotomy
- Argumentation
- Graphic models

Of these, only reflection does not lend itself to capturing the synthesis on a worksheet.

Reflection

All eight synthesis methods involve reflective thinking, but here I emphasize reflection as a distinct method for considering a subject matter with the goal of seeing it in its "right" relations.

The products of reflective thinking are likely to be a metaphor, a cartoon, a narrative — something that somehow "says it all." Some examples are simple; some are complicated.

Analysts who use reflection as a synthesis method have found their favorite places and times to think. Some walk, some stare out the window, some go to their favorite café and have a cup of coffee. Some think better in the morning; others at night. These reflective thinkers juggle their data until a pattern, an obvious truth, a powerful metaphor, a set of factors, or a detailed formula takes shape in their minds. When they are in control of the conditions under which you think, they are also in control of the quality of your thinking.

Two-Axis Matrix

If analysts have a favorite method of synthesis, it is the two-axis matrix. The usefulness of this method is affirmed by the frequency with which it appears. If we were to pass laws against using the two-axis matrix, both business and education would grind along at a much slower pace. Figure 13.2 provides an example of a two-axis matrix that helps to organize and classify the complex concept of exploitation.

When creating a two-axis matrix, you express one set of variables as a row of descriptive terms on the horizontal axis and the second set as a row of terms on the vertical axis. Where

Figure 13.2. Two-Axis Matrix Showing Equilibrium Among
Potential Exploitative Relationships in Industry and Business.

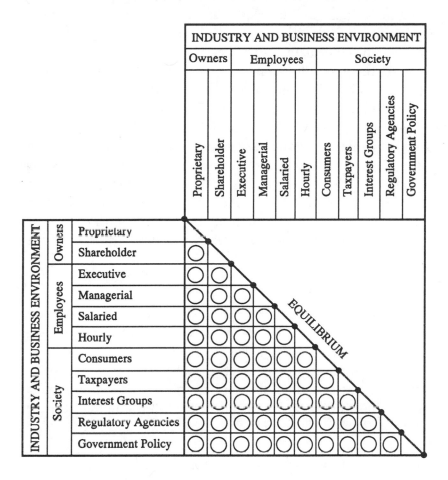

Source: Swanson, 1986.

the two axes cross, cells common to two of the variables are formed. Individual cells may be filled with information or may be void. Either condition should hold some significance for the analyst. A void that should be filled is a clear signal that an important piece of data is missing.

In the Appendix, you will find a two-axis matrix form ready for you to copy. If you think such a worksheet could be used to synthesize your data, use it. Run a trial two-axis matrix synthesis of the subject matter data you have collected. One analyst we know uses the two-axis matrix to organize the content of each piece of research literature he has collected. He simply writes all the titles on one axis and classifies the items of information covered in all the publications on the other axis. Then he checks off the cells by content and information source. The pattern of checks in the matrix cells provides a synthesis of the subject matter.

Three-Axis Matrix

To most of us, the three-axis matrix is not as familiar as the two-axis matrix. It is not flat like the two-axis matrix but is cube shaped — a three-dimensional object. The third axis is most often used to express a set of abstract variables such as judgments of quality, intervals of time, or types of things. Given the large quantity of individual cells produced by even the simplest of these models, it should be clear that the three-axis matrix is a powerful tool for breaking down and reconnecting a very complex subject. Figure 13.3 shows a three-axis matrix used to organize the important area of human resources. Such a model could be used to think about the elements of an organizational human resource function.

The Appendix includes a three-axis matrix form for you to copy and use as a synthesis tool. If you find that working with three-axis matrices is easy for you, be aware that some people are not visually oriented and may have difficulty in mentally slicing this type of matrix into a series of two-axis matrices.

Figure 13.3. Three-Axis Matrix
Depicting a Human Resource Management Cube.

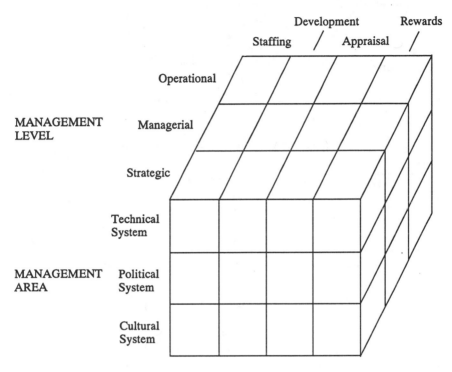

Source: Tichy, 1983. Used by permission.

Flowchart

Flowcharting provides a method for organizing and synthesizing information that contains input-process-output items, decision points, direction of flow, documentation or preparation steps, and confluence and divergence. Some experts and many systems are process oriented. If your subject matter data contains inputs and outputs, try to identify the process elements that belong between them. Figure 13.4 displays a synthesis model of a grievance process for handling incidents of sexual harass-

Figure 13.4. Flowchart Model.

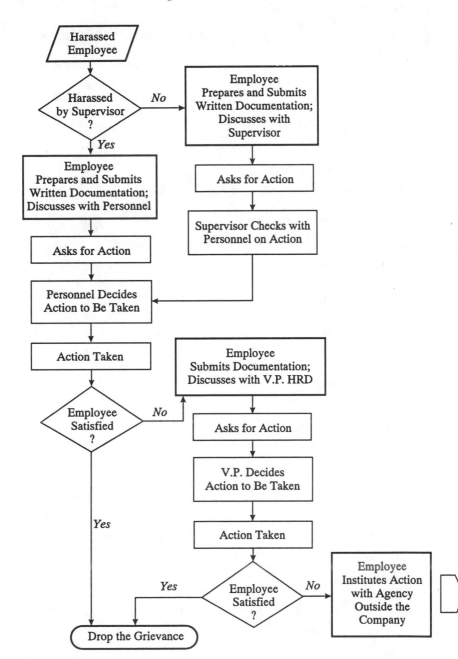

ment in a firm. It clearly shows who is responsible for what, the requirements for documentation, and the end result of not resolving the grievance.

Many subjects that do not appear to lend themselves easily to process-oriented thinking might benefit from such a synthesis. An analyst in a fast-food chain looked at the satisfied customers (outputs) and at the hungry customers (inputs). He used the metaphor of the flow of transactions from the hungry customer to the satisfied customer to synthesize the idea of solving customer problems.

A form showing the flowcharting symbols is available for you to copy and use (see the Appendix). Flowcharting is especially useful for mentally and visually walking through present and future organizational processes or for identifying blocks. Synthesis models of critical processes can lead to better policies and improved decision making in organizations.

Events Network

Time-bound synthesis models that combine all the critical activities and events aimed at the achievement of goals have proven their value to planners, managers, and consultants. Events networks are system oriented. They will help you to take into account all the activity paths and events by which work toward an organizational goal is accomplished. Often such synthesis models are used to describe what should be rather than what is. More than a few subject matter analysts have used events networks to synthesize the masses of information needed for understanding and curing problematic systems. Figure 13.5 shows a simple events network that helped to solve a major organizational problem. It seems that the subscribers deleted were the ones who had just been entered into the records. Certainly, this was no way to run a business, but then no one had made the system visible. Events networks can be made as complicated and precise as necessary. Some will require a huge expanse of fine print to show the lapse of time and the depth and breadth of activities undertaken to reach a goal. Others are computer-

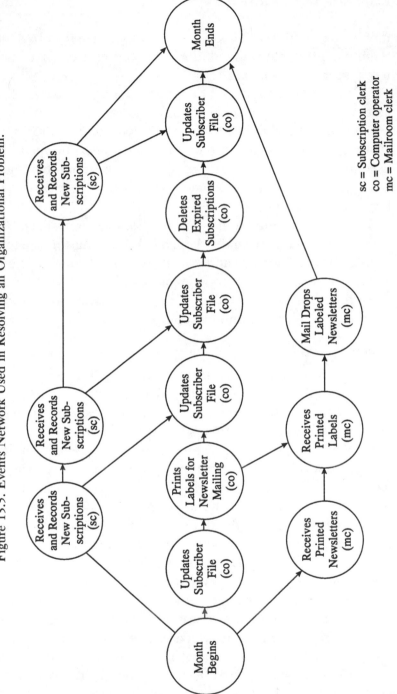

Figure 13.5. Events Network Used in Resolving an Organizational Problem.

sc = Subscription clerk
co = Computer operator
mc = Mailroom clerk

ized and help to calculate the total time and coordination efforts needed for large projects.

The Appendix provides a sample form for constructing an events network.

Dichotomy

One way to approach ambiguous pieces of information is to fit the data into two mutually exclusive groups or camps or contradictory issues. Chris Argyris (1993) used this synthesis method when he subsumed management practice into two categories, *espoused theory* and *theory in use.* He used the model to show managers the contradictions between what they said and what they did.

To work with a diffuse subject area, divide the data into two parts. Good or bad, yes or no, this or that: such dichotomies help to clarify an unclear, undefined subject. Difficult or ambiguous subjects, such as older workers, become more clearly defined when they are synthesized with a dichotomy model (Exhibit 13.1).

Although a dichotomy can be constructed on a sheet of paper folded in half, I have included a sample form in the Appendix. The form will be a reminder to you to use this straightforward but powerful synthesis method.

Argumentation

Some subject matter does not lend itself to argumentation because of the irresolvable nature of the facts. Religion and politics are two cases in point. On the other hand, some seemingly irresolvable issues do lend themselves to reason and dialogue. Argumentation is a synthesis method aimed at resolving two or more theses or positions. The question, "How many angels can dance on the head of a pin?" is not resolvable. But finding an answer to the question, "What is the main societal condition that leads to sexual harassment?" may be possible. For purposes of illustration, I have attempted to do just this (see Exhibit 13.2).

Exhibit 13.1. Dichotomy Example Involving Older Workers.

Facts Related to the Older Worker	Facts Related to the Firm
Background facts — older worker	*Common employer beliefs*
— Over half of all employed Americans want to work past sixty-five — Older workers remain unemployed longer than others — Chronological age is not an indicator of mental or physiological aging — Only half of U.S. workers are covered by a pension plan — Earnings account for 25 percent of money income of elderly — Life expectancy and financial need will keep people in the workforce longer — The job-seeking skills of older workers are often outdated — Career planning programs are increasingly available — Fewer older workers will pay into pension plans and more will draw from them (optional)	— Age is a deterrent to productivity — Jobs are not important to the older worker — Advance in age correlated with diminishing value on the job — Older workers are rigid, inflexible, and unable to compete mentally — Difficult to train older workers *Common blocks to older workers* — Benefits are frozen at age sixty-five — Early retirement is encouraged by greater benefits at an earlier age — Fixed work hours and days limit freedom to do other things — Older workers' experience and skills are not valued — Must retire older workers to make room for younger workers
Older-worker qualities — Superior attendance record — Low accident record — Higher job satisfaction — Eager to learn new skills — Ability to learn continues into old age	*Advantages to the firm that employs older workers* — Older worker by tradition cooperates with co-workers — Reliable work habits — Experience can help firm — Older workers have less turnover — Not so concerned about advancement — Loyalty to the job and the firm — Older worker may pay in, rather than draw on benefits (optional) — Equal or better productivity rates
Reasons older workers continue to work — Financial; not making it on retirement income — Add meaning and purpose to life — Greater social contacts — Identity is tied to work — Look forward to longer life and better health — Use their education	

Exhibit 13.2. Example of Argumentation
Dealing with Sexual Harassment.

ARGUMENTATION

Subject: Sexual Harassment

Analyst:

Major hypothesis: Sexual harassment is a variety of behaviors practiced by the male members of our culture against the female members of our culture.

Supporting facts and assumptions: The many instances of sexual harassment against women can be found in books and in print and broadcast media daily. The practice has harmed and will continue to harm women because policies in the workplace, the law, and the Constitution do not disallow such behaviors.

Counterhypothesis: Sexual harassment is sometimes used against the male members of our culture.

Supporting facts and assumptions: It is true that many men have reported incidents of being harmed by sexual harassment that was perpetrated by both men and women. This practice would seem to contradict the contention that sexual harassment is the result of a cultural bent against women.

Resolution: The real issue is one of power. Men and women need to raise each other's awareness and to counter past and current views of persons as property, as objects to serve at the pleasure of those in greater power. Whenever women and men collectively organize and demand respect for their persons and their self-esteem and then work to aim all persons in society toward courtesy and fairness, sexual harassment will no longer be an acceptable behavior for anyone, no matter how powerful.

Like the dichotomy technique, the argumentation method explores two opposing facets of an issue. Argumentation requires that you pose a best possible hypothesis and its supporting logic. You then disengage from this first hypothesis and propose a counterhypothesis with which to attack and test your first hypothesis. This intellectual attack provides the basis for modifying and refining the original hypothesis. The process ends with a resolution to the argument. Classical debate is a prime example of argumentation. The parties to a debate must attack their own arguments intellectually before those arguments are torn apart by their opponents.

Again, a simple sheet of paper with headings is all that is needed to complete an argumentation. I have included a form in the Appendix to remind you that argumentation may be an appropriate synthesis tool for your subject.

Graphic Models

Organizational charts, product-life-cycle diagrams, maps—these can be circular, spiral, triangular, treelike, wheel shaped—the sky is the limit when it comes to graphic models. When analysts capture the subject matter in a particularly fitting graphic model, it is easily understood. Such models have an appealing, visual quality that stays with even the most casual viewer. The performance taxonomy triangle (Figure 5.7) exemplifies the simple, visual, inclusive qualities of a memorable graphic-synthesis model. For the analyst who thinks visually, the triangle could have come first to the mind's eye or through doodling on paper.

Linear graphic models are particularly useful for depicting the steps or phases of a process. I created simple linear models to organize and synthesize the subject matter of this book. The difference between a linear model and a flowchart model is important. While the flowchart includes decision points, the linear model does not. In the linear model, no step is missed or skipped. All steps are experienced. Linear models can be used to capture the thinking processes of expert performers such as loan officers.

When you must create a synthesis model showing the qualities, quantities, and directions of interactions between people or machines, a graphic interaction model is appropriate. The transactional nature of much of organizational life lends itself to the use of heavy and light, dotted or dashed arrows—whatever will help to synthesize the meaning of the transactions.

The form for graphic modeling in the Appendix is simply a blank page with sample illustrations in the frame. This form has been included to remind you to unleash your creative faculties whenever you synthesize a subject matter graphically. Aim to make the "thousand words" of your graphic model say something important about your subject.

Caution: Although the diversity of graphic modeling offers great freedom to the subject matter analyst, far too many graphic synthesis models confuse rather than clarify. Just because a graphic model works well for you does not mean that it will work for others. Therefore, the model should not always be carried forward to the subject matter description step.

Which Synthesis Model?

Finding a synthesis model for a given collection of information about a subject matter is difficult work made easier by having good tools. Unlike the expert who uses only one or two favorite synthesis models, you now have many models from which to choose. Thus, the likelihood of your finding a model that best fits your data is increased. Finding a truly elegant model — one about which people say "Of course, how could it be any other way?" — requires creativity of the highest order.

Subject Matter Description

You have collected information, analyzed it, and synthesized it. The final step in the process of analyzing knowledge tasks is writing the subject matter description, an orderly presentation of all the important, job-relevant information on a given subject. You may or may not decide to include your synthesis model in the subject matter description. In any event, this model serves a useful purpose as the organizing framework for presenting the information. Exhibit 13.3 contains a knowledge task analysis of sexual harassment — a subject matter description based on several synthesis models.

For credibility, the subject matter description ends with a list of references and other sources of information that were actually used in the final description — not every article or book you have read. The last page of the same subject matter description lists the resources used.

Exhibit 13.3. Example of Subject Matter
Description Focusing on Sexual Harassment.

Subject Matter Description

Job or Program <u>Sexual Harassment Policies and Responses</u>	Page <u>1</u> of <u>6</u>
Location <u>St. Paul</u>	Effective Date <u>5/29/94</u>
Department <u>Companywide</u>	Cancels Sheet Dated <u>N/A</u>
Analyst <u>D. Gradous</u>	Approved by <u>B. Williams</u>

Task: Responding to Sexual Harassment

Performance Standard: To ensure legal compliance on the part of the company and to install knowledge policies and procedures for discouraging and handling sexual harassment.

I. Sexual Harassment is defined in several ways.
 A. It takes the form of jokes, innuendos, remarks, references to women's anatomy, whistles, catcalls, or deliberately eyeing a woman up and down.
 B. Men don't perceive sexual harassment the same as women do, perhaps because of their cultural conditioning, their denial, or their lack of awareness of women's issues.
 C. The *Harvard Business Review* survey of 1980 revealed that:
   1. Women may expect differential and less supportive treatment in the workplace—the men will stick together and cover for one another.
   2. Men blame the women, saying that women provoke harassment by their actions or their manner of dress.
   3. Managers tend to ignore or to deny that any incidents of harassment have occurred within areas for which they are responsible; they may warn or otherwise protect the offender, whom they value as one of the team.
 D. The Equal Employment Opportunity Commission has issued guidelines for executive action about sexual harassment. Sexual harassment is:
   1. "A prohibited personnel practice when it results in discrimination or action against an employee on the basis of conduct not related to performance.
   2. "Deliberate or repeated unsolicited verbal comments, gestures, or physical actions of a sexual nature that are unwelcome. Within the federal government, a supervisor who uses implicit or explicit coercive sexual behavior to control, influence, or affect the career, salary, or job of an employee is engaged in sexual harassment." (federal policy 1979)
   3. Unwanted behavior on the part of one person toward another, generally taking place out of public view.
   4. Unwelcome conduct of a sexual nature in the work environment that threatens one's person or one's position in the organization.
   5. Ranges from looks or verbal innuendos to explicit sexual demands linked to performance evaluation and keeping one's job.

Exhibit 13.3. Example of Subject Matter Description Focusing on Sexual Harassment, Cont'd.

Subject Matter Description

Job or Program __Sexual Harassment Policies and Responses__	Page _2_ of _6_
Location __St. Paul__	Effective Date __5/29/94__
Department __Companywide__	Cancels Sheet Dated __N/A__
Analyst __D. Gradous__	Approved by __B. Williams__

    6. Verbal threats or abusive comments, leers, and nonaccidental touching.

    7. Jokes, obscenities, and double entendres about women and directed at women workers.

    8. Regulations requiring women to wear provocative costumes at work and *not* making the same requirement of men.

    9. Behavior that demeans, confuses, embarasses, and intimidates.

    10. Any sexually oriented practice that undermines a person's job performance or threatens economic livelihood.

  E. Sexual harassment is not:

    1. Mutual sexual behavior between consenting adults who happen to work in the same organization. (Such behavior between persons of unequal status is open to the question of coercion.)

    2. Making a fuss over an office romance that has ended.

    3. Being embarassed or feeling the tension of sexual attraction to another person and choosing not to act on it.

II. Sexual harassment can be seen as an issue of power.

  A. Harassment is by definition integrated within a social context in which women as a group have a disproportionately small share of wealth and authority and social advantages compared to men as a group.

  B. As power increases, the perceived ability to act on one's wishes without suffering the consequences increases.

  C. Persons in hierarchical positions of authority (usually men) can use their roles to place conditions of compliance (sexual or otherwise) on their subordinates.

  D. In hierarchies, where there are power differentials, top management may fail or refuse to see the destructive actions of subordinates — actions that result in high turnover rates and that fail to make use of the full competencies of 40 percent of the workforce.

  E. Women must use energy to fend off unwanted behaviors instead of applying their capacities to performance on the job.

  F. Sexual harassment may be seen as a power play, a conscious or unconscious way of expressing authority and dominance.

  G. *Harvard Business Review* readers rate supervisors' behaviors as more serious and threatening than the same behaviors by peers.

  H. Men conspire to keep silent about one another's conduct in this area — the power to obscure or deny reality.

III. Some believe that the sexual harassment issue is a side issue.

  A. Many fear that this issue might get in front of other minority rights issues.

Exhibit 13.3. Example of Subject Matter
Description Focusing on Sexual Harassment, Cont'd.

Subject Matter Description

Job or Program __Sexual Harassment Policies and Responses__	Page _3_ of _6_
Location _____St. Paul_____	Effective Date _____5/29/94_____
Department ____Companywide____	Cancels Sheet Dated __N/A__
Analyst _____D. Gradous_____	Approved by _____B. Williams_____

    B. Some say that at least a few women ask for such treatment through a desire for some personal advantage such as a promotion or special favors.

    C. At least *one* woman has been found guilty and punished for sexually harassing aman.

    D. Some say this exemplifies the power of a special interest group to exaggerate the importance of a minor reality.

    E. Cries of sexual harassment could be used as a defense to cover issues of incompetence and poor work performance.

IV. Sexual harassment can be traced throughout the history of the human race.

    A. Contrary to anthropologists' claims, the lifestyle of the cave dwellers may not have depended on the superior strength of the male hunters so much as on the steady food gathering behaviors of the females.

    B. In the Middle Ages, lords claimed the "right of first night" with the brides of their serfs.

    C. Slave owners often shared their women slaves with male visitors.

    D. Women working in cottage industries were dependent on the goodwill of middlemen who brought them supplies and picked up the finished goods—men who threatened the women with cutting their supplies or with bringing inferior materials, and so on.

    E. During the Industrial Revolution, women in factories were denied privacy to go to the bathroom and then were blamed for unseemly behavior.

    F. In 1915, Carrie Davis, a housemaid, shot her employer because he "ruined her character."

    G. From 1950 to 1965, women worked in the "pink ghetto" as waitresses, sales clerks, and office workers and suffered sexual harassment in silence—this after being welcomed as workers during World War II.

V. The action against sexual harassment beings.

    A. In 1964, the Civil Rights Act made sex discrimination illegal and sexual harassment came to be seen as a subissue of discrimination.

    B. In 1976, *Redbook* magazine surveyed its readers on the subject of sexual harassment and experienced an avalanche of replies.

    C. In 1978, Judge Finesilver found Johns-Manville guilty of permitting sexual harassment in the workplace.

    D. In 1980, the Equal Employment Opportunity Commission issued

Exhibit 13.3. Example of Subject Matter
Description Focusing on Sexual Harassment, Cont'd.

Subject Matter Description

Job or Program __Sexual Harassment Policies and Responses__	Page _4_ of _6_
Location __St. Paul__	Effective Date __5/29/94__
Department __Companywide__	Cancels Sheet Dated __N/A__
Analyst __D. Gradous__	Approved by __B. Williams__

guidelines defining and outlawing sexual harassment in the workplace.

VI. Many of the legal solutions for sexual harassment are costly and relatively ineffective.
   A. Under Section 703 of Title VII of the Civil Rights Act of 1964, which prohibits discriminatory employment practices based on race, sex, religion, or national origin, only a handful of suits have been tried.
   B. The EEOC guidelines of April 1980 define and prohibit sexual harassment for private employers of fifteen or more employees and all federal, state, and local government workers.
   C. Harassed persons may file civil suits under tort law because employers are deemed responsible for the actions of their employees; however, strong prevention programs by employers may mitigate against collecting damages.
   D. In the case of rape or assault, the employer may be held responsible for failing to provide a safe place to work.
   E. In Minnesota today when a woman files a civil suit and it is her word against his, she is presumed to be telling the truth of her experience of sexual harassment.
   F. The law is male oriented and may perceive certain male behaviors to be socially acceptable.
VII. Collective action by women is possible.
   A. In 1977, Working Women United Institute was formed as a network for referrals, legal advice, and job counseling service for victims of sexual harassment.
   B. Picketing and leafleting to expose sexual harassment (public embarassment) are somewhat effective in convincing management that this is a personnel issue.
   C. Unions represent at least the potential for protection by providing sanctions through the contracting process.
VIII. Action internal to an organization is possible.
   A. Organizational leaders can establish policies, guidelines, and grievance processes to limit sexual harassment in the workplace.
   B. Such policies must cover all types of harassment.
   C. The grievance process must be simple and visible to encourage legitimate complaints.
   D. To assure effectiveness, the Chief Executive Officer must endorse

Exhibit 13.3. Example of Subject Matter
Description Focusing on Sexual Harassment, Cont'd.

Subject Matter Description

Job or Program __Sexual Harassment Policies and Responses__	Page __5__ of __6__
Location __St. Paul__	Effective Date __5/29/94__
Department __Companywide__	Cancels Sheet Dated __N/A__
Analyst __D. Gradous__	Approved by __B. Williams__

the policies and processes, action must be taken against the of-
fenders, and the victim must be protected against retaliation.
E. The organization must offer support through the process so that the
injured employee does not exit the organization or seek outside support before exhausting internal steps.
F. Documentation on the part of the victim is essential because it forces
the organization to behave responsibly.
G. Women must begin to tell the men they work with that a remark
is not funny, a touch is not welcome, and a gesture is not appropriate, but they will not do so unless organizational policies support and
make clear what behaviors *are not* permitted.

Exhibit 13.3. Example of Subject Matter
Description Focusing on Sexual Harassment, Cont'd.

Subject Matter Description

Job or Program _Sexual Harassment Policies and Responses_	Page _6_ of _6_	
Location _St. Paul_	Effective Date _5/29/94_	
Department _Companywide_	Cancels Sheet Dated _N/A_	
Analyst _D. Gradous_	Approved by _B. Williams_	

Resource List

Print materials

Backhouse, C., & Cohen, L. *Sexual harassment on the job: How to avoid the working woman's nightmare*. Englewood Cliffs, NJ: Prentice Hall, 1981.

Collins, E. G., & Blodgett, T. B. "Sexual harassment . . . some see it . . . some won't." *Harvard Business Review*, March-April 1981, pp. 77–94.

Cunningham, M. "Corporate culture determines productivity." *Industry Week*, May 4, 1981, pp. 82–84, 86.

Driscoll, J. B., & Bova, R.A. "The sexual side of enterprise." *Management Review*, July 1980, pp. 51–54.

"Sexual harassment lands companies in court." *Business Week*, October 1, 1979, pp. 120, 122.

Renick, J. C. "Sexual harassment at work: Why it happens, what to do about it." *Personnel Journal*, August 1980, pp. 658–662.

Rowe, M. P. "Dealing with sexual harassment." *Harvard Business Review*, May-June 1981, pp. 42–44, 46.

Safran, C. "Sexual harassment: The view from the top." *Redbook*, March 1981, pp. 45–51.

Woodrum, R. L. "Sexual harassment: New concern about an old problem." *Advanced Management Journal*, winter 1981, pp. 20–26.

Zemke, R. "Sexual harassment: Is training the key?" *Training*, February 1981, pp. 22, 27–28, 30–32.

Interviews

Fred Gradous, Remmele Engineering, Inc.

Larry Johnson, Dorsey, Windhorst, Hannaford, Whitney, & Halladay

Dixie Lindsey, General Mills, Inc.

Some analysts prefer to develop their subject matter descriptions in full sentences, while others prefer an outline format. A useful description will be complete, meaningfully organized, relevant to the job, and accurate. The key word is *organized.* The information in a subject matter description is logically arranged and accessible. It can be used for guiding performance research, writing a report to management, or providing content for a training program.

Acme Inc.—Analysis of the Knowledge Task of Performing as a Shipping Team Member

The Acme, Inc. case study presented in Chapter Three introduced you to an organization trying to cope with performance problems. Chapter Six included a performance improvement proposal for the Acme Shipping Department. Part of the proposal was a decision to revamp the job of shipper and to train those currently holding the job.

The description of the job of shipper in the Shipping Department of Acme, Inc. was presented in Chapter Nine; the task inventory for the job was included in Chapter Ten. "Process seat cover order" was one of the procedural tasks from the seven-task inventory and was analyzed in Chapter Ten. In Chapter Twelve, a systems task—"Monitor and troubleshoot shipping operations"—was analyzed. Exhibit 13.4 offers an analysis of a shipper's knowledge task: "Perform as shipping team member."

Exhibit 13.4. Example of Shipper's Knowledge Task.

Subject Matter Description

Job or Program: Shipper_____   Page _1_ of _10_

Location: _St. Paul, Minn._____   Effective: _(month/day/year)_____

Department: _Shipping_____   Cancels: _(month/day/year or "None")____

Analyst: _R. Torraco_____   Approved: _(supervisor or department head)_

Task: #6—Perform as Shipping Team Member

Performance Standard
When confronted with difficult substitution problems, shipping process problems, or short-falls in daily production, shippers will work in teams to remedy the problems using the Plan-Do-Check-Act Cycle.

---

1. Definitions of *team, teamwork,* and *team building.*
   A. A *team* is a group of people who have as their highest priority the accomplishment of team goals. This is contrasated with a nonteam, which tends to be a group of people with personal agendas that are more valuable to the individuals than to the group as a whole. Teams are characterized by members who support each other, collaborate freely, and communicate openly and clearly with one another.
   B. Common kinds of teams:
      (1) *Committees* usually serve as investigative or advisory bodies reporting to the person or agency that has appointed or organized them.
      (2) *Task forces* are temporary problem-solving groups formed to deal with issues or projects that cross functions or lines of authority. A task force may, for its life, be full time or part time.
      (3) *Process improvement teams* are groups of employees and supervisors who identify and solve problems to increase the effectiveness of their work groups through improved quality and higher productivity (adapted from Quick, 1992).
   C. *Teamwork* is a method by which two or more people accomplish work. It is characterized by collaboration, shared bases of power and decision making, clear and open methods for communicating and dealing with conflict, and consensus on the goals to be achieved.
   D. *Team building* is the attempt to assist the work group to become more adept at its own problems by learning, with the help of a process consultant, to identify, diagnose, and solve its own problems (Baker, 1979).
   E. *Team building* is a set of activities whereby members of a work team:
      (1) begin to understand more thoroughly the nature of group dynamics and effective teamwork, particularly the interrelationship of process and content, and
      (2) learn to apply certain principles and skills of group process toward greater team effectiveness (Burke, 1982).

Exhibit 13.4. Example of Shipper's Knowledge Task, Cont'd.

Subject Matter Description

Job or Program: Shipper _____   Page _2_ of _10_

Location: St. Paul, Minn. _____   Effective: (month/day/year) _____

Department: Shipping _____   Cancels: (month/day/year or "None") _____

Analyst: R. Torraco _____   Approved: (supervisor or department head) _____

2. The benefits and importance of teamwork.
   A. Teamwork results in benefits both for the members of a team and for the organization in which they work. Collaboration — people working well together and supporting one another — is a primary benefit of teamwork.
   B. Improved communication is a benefit of teamwork. Team members communicate openly with information flowing freely in all directions — up, down, and laterally.
   C. Teamwork allows a more efficient application of resources and talents to identifying and solving problems. With the cooperation and pooling of resources by team members, whenever one member lacks resources or expertise, another member is there to pick up the slack. Open communication prevents duplication of effort.
   D. Quality improvement is often the result of teamwork. Team membership instills team pride in members, and they want to make the team look as good as possible. Solving work problems using teamwork, decision making based on data, and the support of top management can result in tangible improvements in quality.
3. Prerequisites for successful teamwork include the following:
   A. Teamwork and team-building efforts must be supported by top management. The organizational culture must reflect a democratic style of leadership.
   B. Successful teams require the support and commitment of the formal team leader(s). Team leaders must have expertise in team building and in all phases of team development.
   C. Team members must want involvement in teams — that is, participation in teams must be voluntary, not through involuntary assignment.
   D. Teams are more highly motivated if they are currently facing problems. Conversely, teams lose focus and interest in the absence of problems requiring solutions.
   E. Successful teams require adequate time for team development (approximately a year) and adequate time to accomplish their prescribed goals.
4. The stages of team growth (adapted from Scholtes, 1988).
   A. *Forming.* This initial stage is characterized by a transition from individual to team member status and by the formal and informal testing of the team leader's guidance. At team formation, there may be

Exhibit 13.4. Example of Shipper's Knowledge Task, Cont'd.

Subject Matter Description

Job or Program: __Shipper__	Page __3__ of __10__
Location: __St. Paul, Minn.__	Effective: __(month/day/year)__
Department: __Shipping__	Cancels: __(month/day/year or "None")__
Analyst: __R. Torraco__	Approved: __(supervisor or department head)__

feelings of pride in team membership, feelings of anxiety, fear, and suspicion about what lies ahead, as well as some anticipation and optimism about the team's capabilities.

B. *Storming.* This is likely the most difficult stage for the team. Members realize the task is different and perhaps more difficult than they expected. Not yet exhibiting true teamwork, members rely solely on individual experience rather than collaboration to address problems. Other behaviors exhibited during the storming phase include resistance, defensiveness, questioning the selection of the project and of the other members who appear on the team, disunity among members, and lack of consensus on the purpose and goals for the group.

C. *Norming.* Initial tension and competition are replaced by acceptance of the team, acceptance of individual roles and membership on the team, and relief that everything is apparently going to work out. As members begin to confide in each other and identify common experiences, a sense of trust and team cohesion begins to develop. Team members collectively establish team ground rules and boundaries (the "norms"), and finally the group can begin to make significant progress in addressing the project.

D. *Performing.* At this point, members have discovered each other's strengths and weaknesses and begin to exhibit a collaborative approach to solving problems. Change necessary for team progress is more readily identified and implemented. Since the team now has the ability to prevent or work through obstacles to performance, work is being done and group goals are beginning to be achieved. Members feel pride and satisfaction at the team's progress.

5. Team-building roles (adapted from Quick, 1992).

A. *Supporting.* As the team develops, there is a realization that support and encouragement of other members results in more and better contributions from them. Mutual support among members leads to an increased sense of self-worth and enhanced team performance.

B. *Confronting.* It is not uncommon for an individual's behavior to be detrimental to team progress. One member may attempt to prevent or discredit the contributions of another. Unkind comments about members or their ideas may surface. Team members can constructively confront this undesirable behavior, as long as the confrontation

Exhibit 13.4. Example of Shipper's Knowledge Task, Cont'd.

Subject Matter Description

Job or Program: __Shipper_____   Page __4__ of __10__

Location: __St. Paul, Minn._____   Effective: __(month/day/year)_____

Department: __Shipping_____   Cancels: __(month/day/year or "None")_____

Analyst: __R. Torraco_____   Approved: __(supervisor or department head)_____

is confined to the *undesirable behavior* and not directed at the offender's *personality*.

C. *Gatekeeping.* At times, group dynamics are such that certain members monopolize a discussion so completely that others can't enter it or are so intimidated that they remain silent. In this case, a *gatekeeper* may say to monopolizers, "You have clearly expressed quite a number of ideas. I'd like to hear what some others have to say. For example, Carol appears to have something she wishes to say."

D. *Mediating.* Intense or prolonged disagreement can occur during interactions among team members. When disagreement between members becomes so polarized that they can't move toward each other's point of view, mediation between the members is needed. Another team member acting as the mediator intervenes to illuminate and clarify each point of view. First, the mediator asks for permission from opposing members to interpret their positions, and then does so for each side of the argument. After clarification, the mediator asks if the clarified versions reflect each disputant's argument. Each member then has an opportunity to revise or correct what was said. This often clarifies real differences or areas of disagreement that may not have been acknowledged. When team members get stuck in personal disagreements, mediation can break the impasse and move discussions forward.

E. *Summarizing.* During group problem-solving sessions, it is not uncommon for groups to get lost in details and become confused as to the overriding issue or problem. During such confusion, a team member intervenes to sum up what has been discussed so far. This summary allows the group to reframe the real question to be answered and restores confidence in the group's purpose. Other members may add to the summary and provide additional data on which further work can be based.

F. *Process observing.* The "processing" of group interaction is a review of what the group is doing effectively and what the group is doing ineffectively. The process observer is usually a facilitator who provides members with feedback, both positive and negative, about how they are functioning as a team. "Process" information highlights the team's strengths and weaknesses and allows the team to improve its effectiveness.

Exhibit 13.4. Example of Shipper's Knowledge Task, Cont'd.

Subject Matter Description

Job or Program: __Shipper__   Page __5__ of __10__

Location: __St. Paul, Minn.__   Effective: __(month/day/year)__

Department: __Shipping__   Cancels: __(month/day/year or "None")__

Analyst: __R. Torraco__   Approved: __(supervisor or department head)__

---

6. Team-subverting roles (adapted from Quick, 1992).
    A. *Shutting off.* Shutting off is a way that one member can quickly silence another. Through interruption or at a pause in discussion, the speaker is ignored or contradicted by another member. The speaker often responds to shutting-off behavior with anger or withdrawal. Because of the personal animosity it engenders, this behavior has a destructive effect on team-building efforts.
    B. *Dominating.* Domination is a common obstacle to the effective functioning of teams. The member in the role of dominator wants to take over the team discussion and may be heavy-handed in his or her efforts to do so. The major obstacle to the continued effectiveness of the team is that the dominator is more interested in pursuing personal agendas than in achieving the team's goals. If the dominator succeeds in monopolizing the team discussion, participation of other members will noticeably decline.
    C. *Labeling.* Labeling is the practice of putting a label on behavior or suggesting that another member has a particular attitude or unworthy motive. Labeling is very counterproductive to team progress because it elicits defensiveness and negative feelings among team members. Labeling can sidetrack useful discussions and even cause a team discussion to be terminated.
    D. *Naysaying.* Unfortunately, the power of no often has disproportionate weight in many team deliberations. The team may be considering an option or proposal that has merit but that may also be unusual or risky. In this situation, the team may be susceptible to the naysayer who, for whatever reason, is opposed to idea and provides the team with a reason for abandoning it. Naysaying is a shortsighted and counterproductive behavior. For the moment, it allows the team to escape from meaningful decision making.
7. Elements and practices of successful teams.
    A. The problem-solving process can become more productive in the following ways:
        (1) Keep the group small. Full participation is more readily achieved in a small group than in a large group. Experts recommend that optimum group size is between five and nine members (Quick, 1992).
        (2) Create a plan for team action with input from members. The

Exhibit 13.4. Example of Shipper's Knowledge Task, Cont'd.

Subject Matter Description

Job or Program: _Shipper_   Page _6_ of _10_

Location: _St. Paul, Minn._   Effective: _(month/day/year)_

Department: _Shipping_   Cancels: _(month/day/year or "None")_

Analyst: _R. Torraco_   Approved: _(supervisor or department head)_

---

    team's action plan sets a timetable for achieving team objectives and determines what advice, assistance, materials, training, and other resources the team will need.

    (3) Announce team meetings in advance. Define the issue to be addressed at the meeting and encourage members to come prepared with ideas and possible solutions. Individual preparation maximizes the time and energy for *group* work and decision making.

    (4) Groups are generally better at evaluating ideas than generating them; individuals are better at coming up with ideas. Encourage members to discuss an idea with the group, not with the originator. Other members should not put undue pressure on the originator to defend or argue for the idea.

    (5) Team members should have cues or reminders about the objectives toward which the team is working. Timely agendas or key words that have meaning for the group should be referred to or made visible in the team's work area.

B. Optimal group dynamics and teamwork can be developed in the following ways:

    (1) Achieve consensus on team goals. The goals of the team should be consistent with its original mission. Goals should be clarified and discussed until full consensus among members is achieved. Unacceptable or unworkable goals must be modified or eliminated from the team's agenda.

    (2) Establish basic guidelines for team behaviors. Team members should agree on a few basic guidelines for how members will work together as a group. Written guidance clarifies what behaviors the group considers desirable versus those it considers unacceptable. For example, a broad range of ideas and opinions should be encouraged, while individual domination of discussion and criticism of other members should be identified as unacceptable.

    (3) Define the roles of team members. Once the talents, experiences, and interests of team members are apparent, work will proceed most efficiently if team roles are clearly defined. The roles of team leader, facilitator, technical expert(s), quality advisor, and others must be formally designated.

    (4) Encourage discussion and constructive criticism of ideas and proposals. If necessary, rephrase criticism in a positive way. The

Exhibit 13.4. Example of Shipper's Knowledge Task, Cont'd.

Subject Matter Description

Job or Program: Shipper   Page 7 of 10

Location: St. Paul, Minn.   Effective: (month/day/year)

Department: Shipping   Cancels: (month/day/year or "None")

Analyst: R. Torraco   Approved: (supervisor or department head)

---

nature of criticism is such that it is often expressed in negative terms. Yet critical thinking is needed to reach team goals.

(5) As an integral part of group development, all team members should achieve awareness of the group process and experience their own sense of responsibility for team progress. All team members are accountable for team*work* and for contributing to the achievement of group goals. Any member can intervene to correct a problem in how the team is functioning. The team's process and outcomes are the responsibilities of each individual member (adapted from Scholtes, 1988).

8. Evaluating and rewarding teamwork.

A. The team's performance must be based on the progress of the team against agreed-on goals, *not* on the activity of individual members. Evaluation of performance that is activity based gives a self-defeating message: that the *results* of teamwork are not important! Evaluation should encourage collaboration and teamwork. Team performance can be evaluated in several ways.

(1) The team as a whole should track their progress against the objectives they have established. This occurs most effectively when *progress charts* based on the initial objectives and timetable are regularly assessed and updated by the team.

(2) The performance of individual team members can be evaluated by peers. Peer evaluation is valuable because members are knowledgeable about the impact of the behavior of others. Peer evaluation can be both written and oral and can occur individually or through a group evaluation session. The advantage of a group setting is that all team members are present to hear feedback and are free to ask a member-evaluator why they have been given a particular assessment of performance. Of course, a disadvantage of evaluation in group settings is that a member who receives several unfavorable performance assessments may feel threatened and react negatively to an open evaluation.

(3) The most commonly used method is evaluation of the individual member by the team leader. This is based on the traditional model of performance appraisal where feedback on performance comes primarily from a single evaluator. This method carries with it the biases of evaluator perceptions (for example, "halo effects"),

Exhibit 13.4. Example of Shipper's Knowledge Task, Cont'd.

Subject Matter Description

Job or Program: _Shipper_	Page _8_ of _10_
Location: _St. Paul, Minn._	Effective: _(month/day/year)_
Department: _Shipping_	Cancels: _(month/day/year or "None")_
Analyst: _R. Torraco_	Approved: _(supervisor or department head)_

low recognition of systems effects on individual performance, and other methodological problems.

B. Rewarding successful team performance is a matter of the equitable distribution of rewards *to the team as a whole*. Again, the rewards and reinforcement of performance are based on team output, not individual input. There are many possible ways of rewarding a team for its efforts:

(1) Meaningful praise and recognition of the team from top management.

(2) Monetary and salary rewards; time off from work; new and better furnishings and equipment.

(3) More responsibility and control over the scheduling and performance of work.

(4) Training and development for new or advanced work responsibilities; career opportunities for team members.

(5) Further opportunities for the team to address meaningful work problems.

Exhibit 13.4. Example of Shipper's Knowledge Task, Cont'd.

Subject Matter Description

Job or Program: Shipper	Page 9 of 10
Location: St. Paul, Minn.	Effective: (month/day/year)
Department: Shipping	Cancels: (month/day/year or "None")
Analyst: R. Torraco	Approved: (supervisor or department head)

Resource List

Print Materials

Baker, H. K. (1979). The hows and whys of team building. *Personnel Journal, 58,* 367–370.

Burke, W. W. (1982). *Organization development: Principles and practices.* Boston: Little, Brown.

Dyer, W. G. (1987). *Team building: Issues and alternatives.* Reading, MA: Addison-Wesley.

Quick, T. L. (1992). *Successful team building.* New York: AMACOM.

Scholtes, P. R. (1988). *The TEAM Handbook: How to use teams to improve quality.* Madison, WI: Joiner Associates.

Interviews:

Larry Blomberg, Shipper, Acme, Inc., St. Paul, MN 55101

Ken Kirschner, Shipper, Acme, Inc., St. Paul, MN 55101

Eric Lauderdale, Shipping Supervisor, Acme, Inc., St. Paul, MN 55101

Susan Mancusi, Shipper, Acme, Inc., St. Paul, MN 55101

Ronald Reed, Shipping Supervisor, Acme, Inc., St. Paul, MN 55101

Barbara Jensen, Johnson & Associates, 168 Fifth St., S.E., Minneapolis, MN 55414

Frederick Tracey, Action Consulting Group, 1211 Franklin Blvd., Chicago, IL 60609

Christopher Voeltz, Distribution Manager, ACME Seat Cover Co., St. Paul, MN 55101

Exhibit 13.4. Example of Shipper's Knowledge Task, Cont'd.

Analysis Plan for Knowledge Task

Step 1. Task or Performance Requirement
  • Achieve teamwork and greater
    collaboration among shippers.

Step 2a. Behavioral Search
        Methods and Sources
  • Interview 3 shippers and 3
    managers about teamwork.
  • Consult a teamwork expert.
  • Questionnaire to current and
    former Acme team participants.

Step 3a. Literature Search
        Methods and Sources
  • Review research on teamwork.
  • Read recent teamwork literature.
  • Call industry association for
    information on teamwork, if any.

Step 2b. Analysis Methods
  • Analyze the who, what, when,
    where, how, and why of
    teamwork among shippers.

Step 3b. Analysis Methods
  • Write important ideas from the
    literature in my own words.
  • Include prerequisites, methods,
    and outcomes of successful
    teamwork.

Step 4. Synthesis Model(s)
  • Select and use one or more of
    the methods for synthesizing
    information.

Step 5. Subject Matter
        Description
  • Write a comprehensive,
    detailed outline or narrative
    on teamwork based on the
    analysis and synthesis steps.

Checkpoint

*The following exercise is included so you can check your under-
standing of the procedure used in completing a subject matter
analysis. In the spaces provided, write the letter of the knowledge task analysis step (a–g) that captures the analysis activity
(1–15). Compare your responses to those at the end of the list.*

a.   Task or subject matter

b.   Behavioral search (methods and sources)

c.   Behavioral analysis methods

d.   Literature search (methods and sources)

e.   Literature analysis methods

f.   Synthesis model(s)

g.   Subject matter description (format and features)

___ 1. Decided that some important features of organization
could be shown by a diagram of the numbers and types
of communications between departments.

___ 2. Discarded two articles from among twenty on the topic
of job design because they were written by authors who
did no research.

___ 3. Listed in a well-organized format all that is known about
the potential for job redesign in this organization so that
a coherent report to the vice president could be written.

___ 4. Listed the sources of information so that others could verify
or duplicate the same search and analysis steps.

___ 5. Wrote a complete outline of the information gathered and
organized.

___ 6. Compared the results of twenty interviews.

___ 7. Realized that she had defined eight factors that showed
the vice president was on the right track in challenging
the current organizational design and eight factors that

showed he should take another look before making changes.

___ 8. *The company vice president reported from his performance improvement proposal that "this organization needs some organizing."*

___ 9. *Interviewed many people to find out where in this organization certain policies are developed.*

___10. *Made a two-axis matrix showing the relationships between several dimensions in common among various organizational theories, and the reality of those same dimensions in this organization.*

___11. *Found two books and five articles on organizational theory.*

___12. *Watched an organizational development training film.*

___13. *Examined the differences between the organizational theories of two well-known experts.*

___14. *Sent a questionnaire to 100 employees asking them to identify who makes certain policies in this organization.*

___15. *Checked the results of the employee questionnaire against the results of the interviews.*

Answers
1.f 2.e 3.g 4.g 5.g 6.c 7.f 8.a 9.b 10.f 11.d 12.d
13.e 14.b 15.c

Tips for the Analyst

I did not say that analyzing knowledge work tasks would be easy. Neither do I want to leave you with the impression that the process is too difficult. To succeed as a performance analyst, you will need:

- Perseverance and curiosity to explore many aspects of a subject and performance at work as it relates to that subject

- Research skills for locating information in the literature and in the organization

- An analytical bent for taking information apart and discovering the relationships of the pieces to one another

- The courage to live with ambiguity — you must not feel the need to oversimplify or to pull the data together too soon

- The capacity to tolerate disorder while finding meaning and organization in the data

- The power to organize, combine, limit, and see new arrangements, frames, or ideas in the data

- The ability to synthesize

Conclusion

Knowledge work has become the most critical work in today's economy. Knowledge work requires expertise, not just knowledge. The most important feature of the knowledge task analysis method is the connection of information and theory to expertise and performance.

Whether you are a researcher, manager, trainer, internal auditor, industrial engineer, or consultant, many people in the organization will expect you to be able to analyze a job skillfully. Your ability to analyze and synthesize will establish you as an expert capable of documenting the most complex workplace behaviors.

Chapters Nine through Thirteen have presented the tools for documenting workplace expertise: job description, task inventory, and the three task methods of procedural task analysis, systems task analysis, and knowledge task analysis. Figure 13.6 combines these five subprocesses for an overall process picture of documenting workplace expertise.

Figure 13.6. Overall Process of Documenting Workplace Expertise.

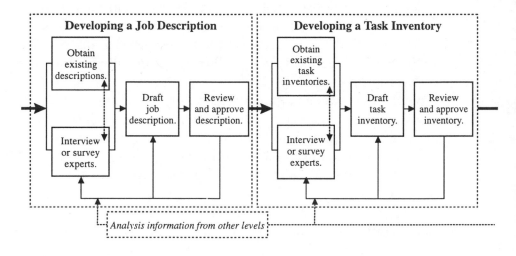

Figure 13.6. Overall Process of Documenting Workplace Expertise, Cont'd.

PART FOUR

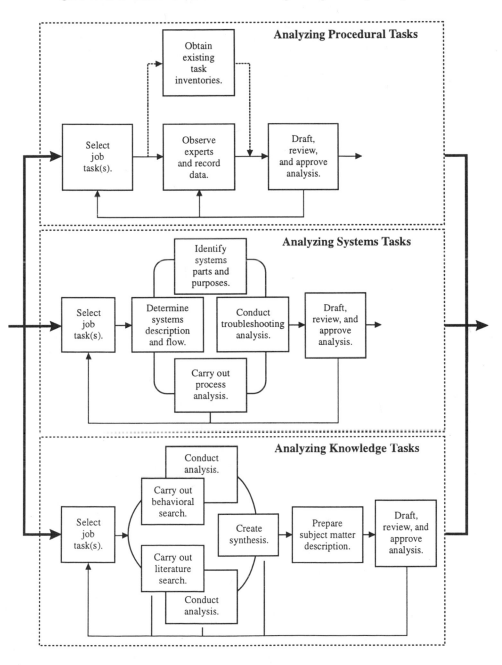

MANAGING
ANALYSIS WORK
TO IMPROVE
PERFORMANCE

Chapter 14

___

Organizing and Prioritizing Analysis Work for Maximum Performance Impact

Analysis for improving performance is a systematic process of diagnosing organizational performance and for analyzing workplace expertise. At the *analysis of organizational performance* level, it offers a five-phase process highlighted by (1) the organizational, process, and individual levels of performance and (2) the performance variables of mission/goal, systems design, capacity, motivation, and expertise. At the *analysis of expertise* level, a five-phase process is used that includes the job description, task inventory, and three unique task analysis tools. Those three task analysis tools have the capability of analyzing the full range of contemporary workplace expertise including knowledge and systems work, not just procedural work.

All the tools presented in this book should now be warmed up and ready to go. However, just because you have them in your toolbox doesn't mean you should use them for every situation. To religiously use all these tools for every performance issue is not recommended. The critics of analysis would argue that the contemporary workplace is so dynamic that investing too much in analysis is foolish. They might suggest jumping from organizational diagnosis, to determining performance requirements, and to hiring workers who have expertise and firing those who are not able to perform at work. This is often an option.

I contend that much of the work that is labeled *changing and fluid* is simply the result of poorly defined work systems and less-than-expert workers. As mentioned earlier, jobs and the inventory of job tasks typically get shuffled at a rate that exceeds the change in requirements within the tasks that are being reassigned. Organizations, processes, and jobs are less stable than workplace tasks. If there is no documentation surrounding the task and it is reassigned to another worker, that expertise is in danger of being lost to the organization. These losses are being experienced day in and day out by large and small organizations. The accumulated performance losses are enormous. The application of performance diagnosis and documentation of workplace expertise should put an organization on the path to improving its situation.

I also contend that changing requirements should not force an organization into hiring and firing as the only means of staying ahead of the competition. Changing organizations may need to create management and human resource systems analogous to flexible manufacturing systems. Flexible management and human resource systems would facilitate having the right people working on the right projects and enrolling the right people in the right development activities. Systematic analysis of workplace expertise would then be focused on the task and task modules that could quickly be configured into job assignments and training programs.

In managing the work of analysis for improving performance, like any other human activity, you should use your judgment about how to handle individual situations. The methods presented in this book have been used successfully in many organizations for diverse purposes. This chapter provides more insight into how to do this by discussing seven principles for managing the analysis. They are as follows:

1.   Defining the performance requirements is half the battle.

2.   Mission and system, system, system.

3. Choose the right tools.
4. Choose the right partners.
5. If it's worth doing, do it!
6. Good solutions make heroes (and good analyses make good solutions).
7. Benefits should exceed costs.

These principles highlight why analysis for improving performance is important, which methods and personnel are best for particular situations, and when a rigorous analysis isn't worth the effort.

Principle 1: Defining the Performance Requirements Is Half the Battle

For most of us, doing the kind of analysis work described in this book requires an understanding of and commitment to performance. If you were not engaged in analysis work, you could easily find other ways to spend your time. So producing an analysis that will not be used is a wasteful way to spend your time.

A clearly confirmed performance requirement establishes the general need for analyzing and documenting workplace expertise. It also offers direction in choosing the appropriate task analysis tools. The following true incident illustrates the necessity for a clearly defined performance requirement:

> The president of XYZ Corporation tells his vice president of operations that he emphatically wants to see a reduction of paper flow in the firm. With a click of his heels, the vice president assembles a task force to reduce paper flow. Their tentative solutions include:
>
> 1. A poster campaign
> 2. Employee newsletter articles
> 3. A work-group discussion program

The president chose the poster campaign. Many four-color posters were designed, produced, and displayed around the facility. The response was nonexistent. Not once did these highly paid corporate sharpshooters ever pin down the president to find out what he meant by paper flow or what types of documents or what level in the organization he was referring to. Whether or not there were important work behaviors that needed to be understood and improved was never resolved. Because the performance issue was never clearly defined, the activity that followed was doomed to failure.

Thus, development and delivery of interventions should be clearly linked to performance requirements. Some situations that would push you toward a clear definition of a performance requirement include:

- Lack of clarity regarding exactly what is actually involved in a work performance situation

- Nonperformance or substandard performance causing critical difficulties in the organization or in the marketplace

- New equipment or new work systems or new employees

- The desire to bring the performance level of all workers up to that of an exemplary performer

- A search for less costly methods of performance being forced by competition

Principle 2: Mission and System, System, System

The perceived performance requirement will start you thinking about what to analyze; the actual performance requirements, as defined by the careful diagnosis, will frame the plan for performance improvement and the possible need to analyze specific workplace expertise. The following items are inherent in all organizations and may yield opportunities to gain surprisingly large benefits from a competent and thorough analysis:

- Corporate culture, or people's attitudes and habits at work
- Equipment use, misuse, maintenance, and their effects on performance
- Work-system analysis and performance improvement
- Personnel policies and practices and their effects on performance
- New technology planning
- Safety issues
- Use of time at work

Quality of analysis for improving performance has its results. The proof is ultimately in the new understanding of performance at work and any resulting solutions that maintain or improve that performance.

Time is the demon in the corporate picture. It seems that the only constant in industry and business is the pressure of time. "Have it done on Monday morning!" is the battle cry. Insufficient time is the most common objection to analysis work — the very analysis work that has the potential to define the specific requirements and work behaviors for significant gains. Thus, analysts who fail to link their analysis work to important performance requirements and to performance results will never make much of a difference to their organizations.

The principle "Mission and system, system, system" highlights the importance of looking at the big picture. You must come to grips with (1) the connection of your role in the organization and (2) the connection of your tools to that role and the tools to each other. A sound mission carried out by a mediocre system that is fully implemented will outstrip the brilliant system that is not honored and worked on a day-to-day basis. Better yet, buy into a best system, master it, honor it, and work it.

Principle 3: Choose the Right Tools

You have learned how to conduct analysis for diagnosing organizations and documenting workplace expertise. Hopefully you have also learned where each tool can most usefully be applied.

Early and conscious estimates as to what analysis tools will be required help you define and control the work. The simple checklist for choosing the right tools for each performance improvement project helps in the initial planning:

__DIAGNOSE PERFORMANCE
    __Articulate Initial Purpose
    __Assess Performance Variables
    __Specify Performance Measures
    __Determine Performance Needs
    __Prepare Performance Improvement Proposal
__DOCUMENT EXPERTISE
    __Prepare Job Description
    __Prepare Task Inventory
    __Conduct Analysis of Procedural Tasks
    __Conduct Analysis of Systems Tasks
    __Conduct Analysis of Knowledge Tasks

The injunction to "Choose the right tool" holds true for all forms of work. It is doubly important for the neophyte. An old craftsperson once said that the newest and best tools are needed by beginners; only skilled old-timers can use less precise or worn tools and still produce good results. If you are new to analysis, carefully choose the most appropriate analysis tools.

Principle 4: Choose the Right Partners

You may be surprised about this one. Too many people in the consulting and performance improvement business want to hold onto their secrets of success and, therefore, restrict participation in their realm of activity.

Never conduct a performance diagnosis by yourself. The person in charge of the organization you are diagnosing should be your partner in managing the diagnosis. Also, think carefully about the need to use unbiased third parties for interviews and surveys. A local consultant or graduate student in performance improvement could be just the right person for some of this work.

In the *best of conditions,* these tools are used in conjunction with experts. However, organizational decisions to implement new processes or work systems can often leave the analyst without a ready expert. The logic of the three task analysis methods helps substitute for the missing expert. Under these conditions the analyst pieces together a variety of "partial experts" to capture the components of expertise. Then the analyst weaves together the components into the complete documentation of expertise required to perform the job and/or its tasks.

The reality is that the tools described in this book can be learned by average people. There have been extraordinary successes in teaching the use of these tools to workers (blue collar and white collar) as well as professional analysts. In one case, a consultant was working with a top management team as partners in diagnosing the organizational performance. Together they flowcharted a core process of a company and identified the fifteen critical jobs within the process. Then expert job incumbents in each job were taught the analysis of expertise tools, and they themselves analyzed the expertise required of each of their own jobs. They didn't think they could do it. Out of fear of failure, they tried to drag the consultant into their workplace. That would have put them in a team mode, with the consultant as analysts and the workers as subject experts. Instead, after teaching them the tools, the consultant withdrew and just stayed in touch via fax machine. They faxed their work to him; he commented on it and faxed it back. It worked. All fifteen of the critical jobs were documented to a high standard in record time.

In another situation, where production waste was sky-high, the workers used the task analysis tools to document the expertise required to do their work. They were going to produce a training program based on the analysis. They did the analysis and as they did it, they learned their jobs. Their production waste went to almost zero, and they ended up not needing to produce training. Doing the analysis produced both learning and an effective job aid.

Many of the horror stories about choosing the wrong people revolve around the overutilization of committees and the utilization of "political appointees." Avoid these options.

Principle 5: If It's Worth Doing, Do It!

Wanting others to do things the right way and wanting them to get it right the first time is a perspective on work held by most work-performance analysts. They should expect no less of themselves.

I am not talking about perfection; perfection is an elusive goal. But excellence is within your reach. Decide to do your best in the time allotted. The old saying "pay now or pay later" could have been written for the analyst. It takes time to do quality analysis, and your boss may not understand why you need to do all that, but let reason prevail. You are the one who will live with the results, so pay now or pay later. I hope you are willing to pay the price for good analysis work and then reap the benefits. Do it!

Principle 6: Good Solutions Make Heroes
(Good Analyses Make Good Solutions)

Analysis for improving performance requires understanding and commitment. By itself, analysis is rarely rewarded. Management rewards solutions, not analysis. Management sees the costs of analysis in time and dollars and the pressing need for solutions. Unfortunately, time is the nemesis of business and industry; therefore, the time for thorough analysis must be snatched from the organization. Taking the time to analyze will ensure good solutions.

Good solutions are grounded in good analysis. More than anyone else in your organization, you understand what it takes to conduct good analyses. Others will neither know nor appreciate the demands of good analysis work. Do not expect management to support your requests for resources without a proven record of delivering on promises of performance improvement.

As a neophyte, you will need to hold your ground in the analysis phase so you can obtain hero status at the solution phase. The major strategies are to (1) focus on present performance problems, (2) have an internal partner that "owns" the performance problem in the diagnosis phase, and (3) wisely use available internal and external resources for both the performance diagnosis and the expertise documentation phases.

Principle 7:
Benefits Should Exceed Costs

Cost analysis by itself is just plain useless. The name of the game in industry and business is cost-benefit analysis—getting a good return on your investment. Table 14.1 provides an example of a cost-benefit chart. Which option would you choose when investing your own money?

Table 14.1. Financial Analysis of Investment Alternatives.

Option	Cost $ (Investment)	Return $ (15 days later)	Return %	Benefit $
A	1.50	1.00	−50	−.50
B	10.00	10.00	0	00.00
C	500.00	600.00	+20	+100.00
D	1,000.00	2,000.00	+100	+1,000.00

Quite frankly, if I didn't have $1,000 readily available, I'd find it quickly so that I could take advantage of the high-cost option D. Options A and B are bad investments. Just because an option is expensive, however, don't think that it's the best. For example:

Table 14.2. Financial Comparison
of Performance Improvement Options.

Option	Cost $	Return $	Return %	Benefit $
A	60.00	180.00	300	+120.00
B	120.00	180.00	150	+60.00
C	300.00	180.00	60	−120.00
D	1,000.00	180.00	18	−820.00

These are real figures from the forecasted costs and benefits of a small performance improvement intervention. The shrewd performance improvement manager went with the low-cost model, not because it was inexpensive, but because of the cost-benefit ratio (Swanson & Gradous, 1988).

The performance analyst in industry and business is a businessperson first and should think as one. If you want to succeed in your organization, you will need to play by the rules of the organization. Knowing what the problems are, what truly constitutes good work performance, and how to link solutions to performance requirements through analysis will be of tremendous value to both you and your organization.

One more bit of advice about the reality of costs and benefits: From this book, you may get the impression that I would like you to analyze all work performance from every angle. This is not so. Excessive or inappropriate analysis can result in paralysis through analysis. Decide when or at what point analysis is not worth the effort. A decision matrix can be useful (see Figure 14.1).

Wouldn't it be great to be able to earn a high return on a low investment? Imagine a tough performance problem in a manufacturing plant—one that results in high waste of an ex-

Figure 14.1. Decision Matrix.

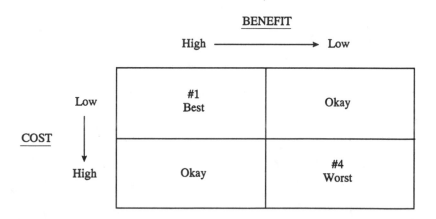

pensive product that is almost totally linked to the lack of worker expertise. You approach the situation through a quick performance diagnosis and the careful analysis of the critical work task. This is then used to efficiently correct the problem. Hero status for you!

If you are new in the organization and must "hit the ground running," a few discrete inquiries will net many identifiable work performance problems. I recommend that you plot all of them on a two-axis, cost-benefit matrix. Wisdom dictates that you choose for your first performance improvement effort one that falls within the low-cost, high-benefit quadrant. If the problem is urgent, so much the better.

Conclusion

It is important to look before you leap into analysis of performance and expertise. My goal has been to provide you with all the tools you need to complete successful, systematic performance diagnosis and documentation of expertise. The potential for return on your investment of time and talent is enormous. Enjoy your analysis expertise and its ability to make a difference in your organization.

Chapter 15

From Analysis
to Performance
Improvement

The journey from analysis to improved performance is one that can be challenging, interesting, and fun. It is almost as rewarding as the final accomplishment. But not everyone feels that way, especially those without a well-equipped analysis toolbox for performance improvement.

Serious scholars in the area of problem solving tell you that the odds of success are increased when you use powerful problem-defining analysis methods. They also tell you that your mental health is enhanced when you are in control of the front-end problem definition. Simply stated, good up-front analysis leads you to success and also helps you feel better about yourself along the way.

Phases of Performance Improvement

The five phases of improving performance were first presented in Chapter Two. They are (1) analyze, (2) design, (3) develop, (4) implement, and (5) evaluate. Figure 15.1 once again illustrates performance improvement as a process that *parallels* and *enhances* core organizational processes (such as product development, customer acquisition, production, and order fulfillment) for the purpose of improving performance.

Figure 15.1. Systems Model of Performance Improvement:
Interacting with Organization Processes.

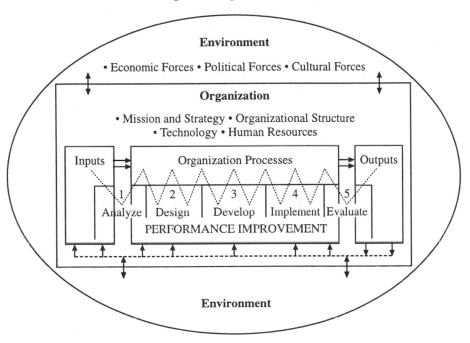

The analysis and evaluation phases of performance improvement connect to the organizational inputs and outputs. Interventions that are not accurately connected to organizational goals at the analysis (input) phase have no chance of finishing the race, let alone of winning the race.

Unfortunately, many organizations learn the importance of analysis after spending large amounts of time and money in the design, development, and delivery phases — only to find that their crowd-pleasing, analysis-less interventions had little or no positive impact on performance.

Interventions such as human resource development, quality improvement, reengineering, and performance technology that are fixated on the design, development, and delivery phases (apart from analysis) are almost always deficient. Each can easily be a sophisticated and costly intervention in search of an ill-defined performance problem — a great solution perhaps to some *other* organization's problem.

Audits of such efforts invariably drive decision makers to ask the question "How did we ever get involved with this?" (Torraco & Swanson, 1991). The answer often is that there was an emotional decision, a hasty decision, a high-pressure sales pitch, or arm twisting from the top.

Performance Variables

To avoid such errors, it is important to emphasize that inside each goal and intervention there are multiple performance variables at work. Thus, the performance variables of mission/goals, systems design, capacity, motivation, and expertise help guide the performance diagnosis, focus the documentation of expertise, *and* help ensure the inclusion of the critical dimensions required of an effective intervention. Being able to positively respond to the questions under each variable enables the performance improvement professional to move closer to success:

Mission/Goal

- Does the organizational mission/goal fit the reality of the economic, political, and cultural forces?

- Do the process goals enable the organization to meet organizational and individual mission/goals?

- Are the professional and personal mission/goals of individuals congruent with the organization's?

Systems Design

- Does the organization system provide structure and policies supporting the desired performance?

- Are processes designed in such a way as to work as a system?

- Does the individual face obstacles that impede job performance?

Capacity

- Does the organization have the leadership, capital, and infrastructure to achieve its mission/goals?
- Does the process have the capacity to perform (quantity, quality, and timeliness)?
- Does the individual have the mental, physical, and emotional capacity to perform?

Motivation

- Do the policies, culture, and reward systems support the desired performance?
- Does the process provide the information and human factors required to maintain it?
- Does the individual want to perform no matter what?

Expertise

- Does the organization establish and maintain selection and training policies and resources?
- Does the process of developing expertise meet the changing demands of changing processes?
- Does the individual have the knowledge, skills, and attitudes to perform?

Conclusion

Analysis is the fuel of performance improvement. Evaluation addresses its ultimate worth. When all is said and done, the conclusion drawn from evaluating a performance improvement intervention should be:

1. The organization performs better.
2. The process performs better.
3. The individual performs better.

Appendix: Master Copies of Diagnosis and Documentation Forms

Exhibit A.1. Job Description Form.

Job Description

Job or Program _____	Effective Date _____
Location _____	Cancels Sheet Dated _____
Department _____	Approved By _____
Analyst _____	

Exhibit A.2. Task Inventory Form.

Task Inventory

Job or Program _____   Page _____ Of _____

Location _____   Effective Date _____

Department _____   Cancels Sheet Dated _____

Analyst _____   Approved By _____

1. _____
2. _____
3. _____
4. _____
5. _____
6. _____
7. _____
8. _____
9. _____
10. _____
11. _____
12. _____
13. _____
14. _____
15. _____
16. _____
17. _____
18. _____
19. _____
20. _____
21. _____
22. _____
23. _____
24. _____

Exhibit A.3. Procedural Task Analysis Form.

Procedural Task Analysis

Job or Program _____	Page ____ Of ____
Location _____	Effective Date _____
Department _____	Cancels Sheet Dated _____
Analyst _____	Approved _____

Task

Performance Standard

Safety and Other Cautions

Major Headings	Sub Headings	Sequential Steps in Performing the Work	Notes*

*Learning Domain: Cognitive = C. Affective = A. Psychomotor = P.   *Learning Difficulty: Easy = E. Moderate = M. Difficult = D.

Exhibit A.3. Procedural Task Analysis Form, Cont'd.

Procedural Task Analysis

Task: (Continued)

Job or Program _____ Page ___ Of ___

Location _____ Effective Date _____

Department _____ Cancels Sheet Dated _____

Analyst _____ Approved _____

Major Headings	Sub Headings	Sequential Steps in Performing the Work	Notes*

*Learning Domain: Cognitive = C. Affective = A. Psychomotor = P.   *Learning Difficulty: Easy = E. Moderate = M. Difficult = D.

Exhibit A.4. Systems Description and Flow Form.

Systems Description and Flow

Job or Program _____	Page ____ Of ____
Location _____	Effective Date _____
Department _____	Cancels Sheet Dated _____
Analyst _____	Approved By _____

Task/System

Systems Purpose/Description:

Exhibit A.5. Systems Parts and Purposes Form.

Systems Parts and Purposes

Job or Program _____	Page ____ Of ____
Location _____	Effective Date _____
Department _____	Cancels Sheet Dated _____
Analyst _____	Approved _____

Task/System

PART Use Correct Name	PURPOSES Explain what the part does. Also explain how it works, if not obvious.

Exhibit A.6. Process Analysis Form.

Process Analysis

Job or Program _____

Location _____

Department _____

Analyst _____

Task/System _____

Effective Date _____

Cancels Sheet Dated _____

Approved By _____

Page ____ Of ____

VARIABLE	SPECIFICATION	INDICATOR	CONTROL	EFFECT OF		OTHER INFORMATION
				PLUS DEVIATION	MINUS DEVIATION	

Exhibit A.7. Troubleshooting Analysis Form.

Troubleshooting Analysis

Job or Program _____	Page ____ Of ____
Location _____	Effective Date _____
Department _____	Cancels Sheet Dated _____
Analyst _____	Approved By _____

Task/System

Performance Standard:

PROBLEM	CAUSE	CORRECTIVE ACTION

Exhibit A.7. Troubleshooting Analysis Form, Cont'd.

Troubleshooting Analysis

Task/System: _____ (continued)

Job or Program _____   Page ____ Of ____

Location _____   Effective Date _____

Department _____   Cancels Sheet Dated _____

Analyst _____   Approved By _____

PROBLEM	CAUSE	CORRECTIVE ACTION

Exhibit A.8. Subject Matter Description Form.

Subject Matter Description

Job or Program _____	Page ____ Of ____
Location _____	Effective Date _____
Department _____	Cancels Sheet Dated _____
Analyst _____	Approved By _____

Task

Performance Standard

Exhibit A.9. Two-Axis Matrix Worksheet Form.

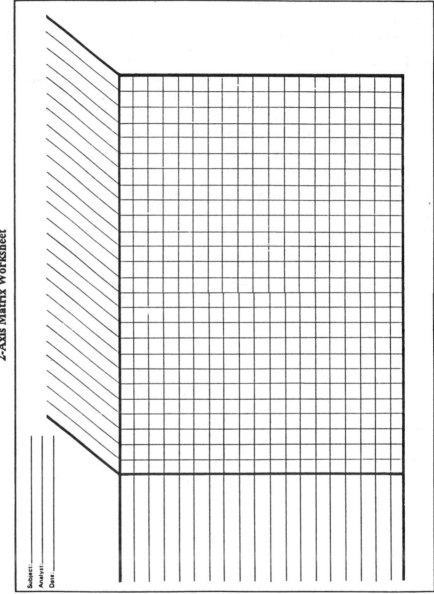

2-Axis Matrix Worksheet

Subject:
Analyst:
Date:

Exhibit A.10. Three-Axis Matrix Worksheet Form.

3-Axis Matrix Worksheet

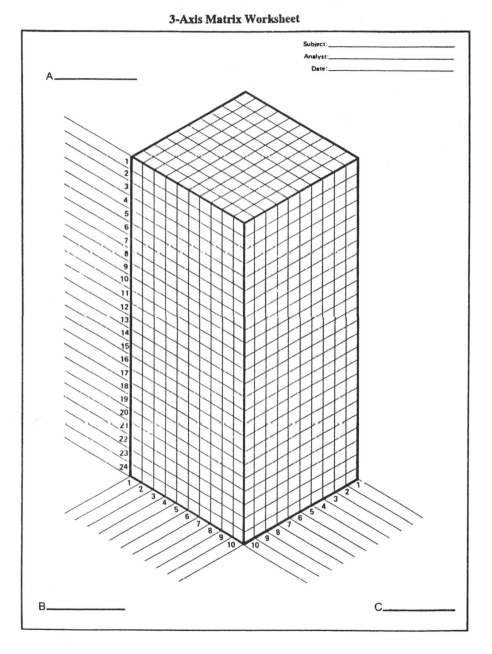

Exhibit A.11. Flowchart Worksheet Form.

Flowchart Worksheet

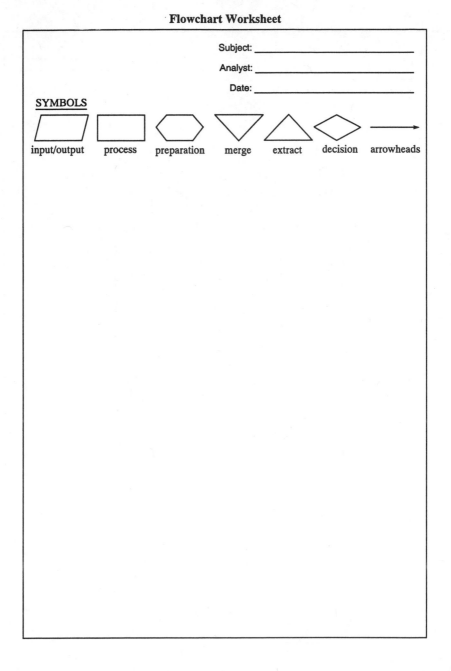

Exhibit A.12. Events Network Worksheet Form.

Events Network Worksheet*

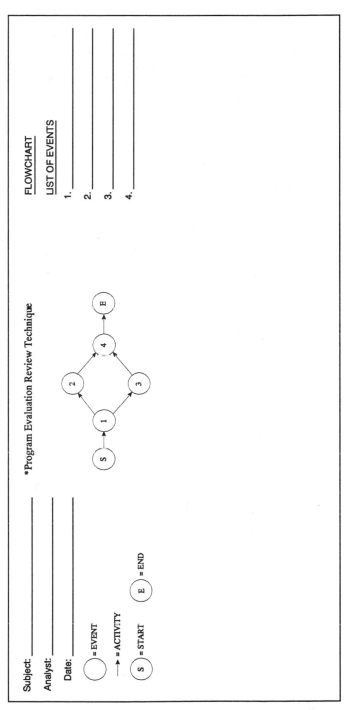

*Program Evaluation Review Technique

◯ = EVENT

—▶ = ACTIVITY

(S) = START   (E) = END

FLOWCHART

LIST OF EVENTS

1. _____

2. _____

3. _____

4. _____

Exhibit A.13. Dichotomy Worksheet Form.

Dichotomy Worksheet

Sample Dichotomous Terms	Subject: _____
good ⟷ bad	Analyst: _____
high ⟷ low	Date: _____
strong ⟷ weak	
structured ⟷ unstructured	
complete ⟷ incomplete	
excellent ⟷ poor	
well ⟷ ill	

(dichotomous term/subject) Part I	Part II (dichotomous term/subject)
_____	_____
Part I: Definition and/or characteristics	Part II: Definition and/or characteristics

Exhibit A.14. Argumentation Worksheet Form.

Argumentation Worksheet

Subject: _____

Analyst: _____

Date: _____

1. MAJOR HYPOTHESIS

Supporting facts and assumptions

2. COUNTERHYPOTHESIS

Supporting facts and assumptions

3. RESOLUTION OF OPPOSING HYPOTHESES

Exhibit A.15. Graphic Modeling Worksheet Form.

Graphic Modeling Worksheet

Subject: _____

Analyst: _____

Date: _____

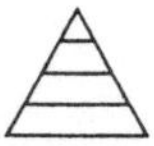

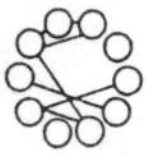

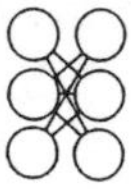

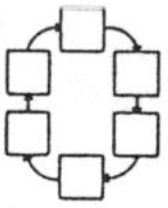

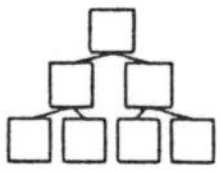

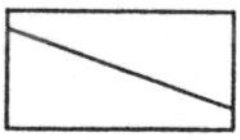

References

Argyris, C. (1993). *Knowledge for action: A guide to overcoming barriers to organizational change.* San Francisco: Jossey-Bass.

Bjorkquist, D. C., & Murphy, B. P. (1987). Teaching how to conduct a needs assessment in industry: Learning by doing. *Journal of Industrial Teacher Education, 24*(2), 32–39.

Boulding, K. E. (1956). General systems theory: The skeleton of a science. *Management Science, 2*(3), 197–207.

Camp, R. C. (1989). *Benchmarking: The search for industry best practices that lead to superior performance.* Milwaukee, WI: ASQC Quality Press.

Campbell, J. P. (1988). Training design for performance improvement. In J. P. Campbell, R. J. Campbell, & Associates, *Productivity in organizations: New perspectives from industrial and organizational psychology* (pp. 177–213). San Francisco: Jossey-Bass.

Campbell, J. P., Campbell, R. J., & Associates. (1988). *Productivity in organizations: New perspectives from industrial and organizational psychology.* San Francisco: Jossey-Bass.

Center for Accelerated Learning. (1992). *Accelerated Learning 1992.* Lake Geneva, WI: Author.

Clarke, D. & Crossland, L. (1985). *Action systems: An introduction to the analysis of complex behavior.* London: Methuen.

Davenport, T. H. (1993). *Process innovation: Reengineering work through information technology.* Boston: Harvard Business School Press.

DuPont. (1989). *ISO 9000 is coming!!! The answers to your questions.* Wilmington, DE: Quality Management and Technology Center, DuPont.

Flanagan, J. C. (1954). The critical incident technique. *Psychological Bulletin, 51,* 327–358.

Fuchsberg, G. (1993). Executive education: Taking control. *Wall Street Journal,* Sept. 10, 1993, pp. R1–R4.

Gilbert, T. F. (1978). *Human competence: Engineering worthy performance.* New York: McGraw-Hill.

Gradous, D. B. (Ed.). (1989). *Systems theory applied to human resource development.* Alexandria, VA: American Society for Training and Development Press.

Hammer, M., & Champy, J. (1993). *Reengineering the corporation: A manifesto for business revolution.* New York: HarperCollins.

Harless, J. H. (1980). *An ounce of analysis is worth a pound of objectives.* Newnan, GA: Harless Press.

Harrington, H. J. (1992). *Business process improvement: The breakthrough strategy for total quality, productivity, and competitiveness.* New York: McGraw-Hill.

Harvey, R. J. (1991). Job analysis. In M. D. Dunnette & L. M. Hough (Eds.), *Handbook of industrial and organizational psychology* (2nd ed., Vol. 2, pp. 71–163). Palo Alto, CA: Consulting Psychologists Press.

Hayes, B. E. (1992). *Measuring customer satisfaction: Development and use of questionnaires.* Milwaukee, WI: ASQC Quality Press.

Jacobs, R. L. (1989). Theory: Systems theory applied to human resource development. In D. B. Gradous (Ed.), *Systems theory applied to human resource development* (pp. 27–60). Alexandria, VA: American Society for Training and Development Press.

Juran, J. M. (1992). *Juran on quality by design: The new steps for planning quality into goods and services.* New York: Free Press.

Kouzes, J. M., & Posner, B. Z. (1987). *The leadership challenge: How to get extraordinary things done in organizations.* San Francisco: Jossey-Bass.

Krueger, R. A. (1988). *Focus groups: A practical guide for applied research.* Newbury Park, CA: Sage.

Kusy, M. (1986). *The effects of type of training evaluation on support of training among corporate managers.* St. Paul: Training and Development Research Center, University of Minnesota.

Lavarakas, P. J. (1987). *Telephone survey methods: Sampling, selection, and supervision.* Newbury Park, CA: Sage.

Lewis, T., & Bjorkquist, D. C. (1992). Needs assessment: A critical reappraisal. *Performance Improvement Quarterly, 5*(4), 33–54.

McLagan, P. A. (1989). Systems model 2000: Matching systems theory to future HRD issues. In D. B. Gradous (Ed.), *Systems theory applied to human resource development: Theory-to-practice monograph* (pp. 61–82). Alexandria, VA: American Society for Training and Development Press.

McLean, G. N. (1988). *Construction and analysis of organization climate surveys.* St. Paul: Training and Development Research Center, University of Minnesota.

Mager, R. F., & Pipe, P. (1984). *Analyzing performance problems.* Belmont, CA: Lake.

Miles, M. B., & Huberman, A. M. (1984). *Qualitative data analysis: A sourcebook of new methods.* Newbury Park, CA: Sage.

Mills, G. E., Pace, W. R., & Peterson, B. D. (1988). *Analysis in human resource training and development.* Reading, MA: Addison-Wesley.

Murphy, B. P., & Swanson, R. A. (1988). Auditing training and development. *Journal of European Industrial Training, 12*(2), 13–16.

Nadler, D. A., Gernstein, M. S., Shaw, R. B., & Associates. (1992). *Organizational architecture: Designs for changing organizations.* San Francisco: Jossey-Bass.

Nadler, L., & Nadler, Z. (Eds.). (1990). *The handbook of human resource development* (2nd ed.). New York: Wiley.

Parker, B. L. (1986). Evaluation in training and development. *Journal of Industrial Teacher Education, 23*(2), 29–55.

Porter, M. E. (1980). *Competitive strategy: Techniques for analyzing industries and competitors.* New York: Free Press.

Rossett, A. (1990). *Training needs assessment.* Englewood Cliffs, NJ: Educational Technology Publications.

Rummler, G. A., & Brache, A. P. (1990). *Improving performance: How to manage the white space on the organization chart.* San Francisco: Jossey-Bass.

Senge, P. M. (1990). *The fifth discipline: The art and practice of the learning organization.* New York: Doubleday.

Senge, P. M. (1993). Transforming the practice of management. *Human Resource Development Quarterly, 4*(1), 5–32.

Sisson, G. R., & Swanson, R. A. (1990, May). Improving work performance. *Educational Technology, 30*(5), 16–20.

Sleezer, C. M. (1991). Developing and validating the performance analysis for training model. *Human Resource Development Quarterly, 2*(4), 355–372.

Sleezer, C. M., & Swanson, R. A. (1992). Culture surveys: A tool for improving organization performance. *Management Decision, 30*(2), 22–29.

Stolovitch, H. D., & Keeps, E. J. (Eds.). (1992). *Handbook of human performance technology: A comprehensive guide for analyzing and solving performance problems in organizations*. San Francisco: Jossey-Bass.

Swanson, R. A. (1981). Analyzing non-observable work behavior. *Journal of Industrial Teacher Education, 18*(4), 11–23.

Swanson, R. A. (1982). High technology, training, and crystal balls. *Criterion*, Nov. 1982, pp. 1–2.

Swanson, R. A. (1985). A business person first. *Performance and Instruction Journal, 24*(7), 10–11.

Swanson, R. A. (1987). Training technology system: A method for identifying and solving training problems in industry and business. *Journal of Industrial Teacher Education, 24*(4), 7–17.

Swanson, R. A. (1989). Everything important in business is evaluated. In R. O. Brinkerhoff (Ed.), *Evaluating training programs in business and industry* (pp. 71–82). *New Directions in Program Evaluation*, no. 44. San Francisco: Jossey-Bass.

Swanson, R. A. (1990). HRD paranormal interventions. *Human Resource Development Quarterly, 1*(3), 207–208.

Swanson, R. A. (1991). Ready-aim-frame. *Human Resource Development Quarterly, 2*(3), 203–205.

Swanson, R. A. (1992a). Demonstrating financial benefits to clients. In H. D. Stolovitch & E. J. Keeps (Eds.), *Handbook of human performance technology: A comprehensive guide for analyzing and solving performance problems in organizations* (pp. 602–618). San Francisco: Jossey-Bass.

Swanson, R. A. (1992b). Pick a system, any system. *Human Resource Development Quarterly, 3*(3), 213–214.

Swanson, R. A., & Gradous, D. B. (1986). *Performance at work: A systematic program for evaluating work behavior*. New York: Wiley.

Swanson, R. A., & Gradous, D. B. (Eds.) (1987). *Adapting human resources to organizational change*. Alexandria, VA: American Society for Training and Development Press.

Swanson, R. A., & Gradous, D. B. (1988). *Forecasting financial benefits of human resource development*. San Francisco: Jossey-Bass.

Swanson, R. A., Horton, G. R., & Kelly, V. (1986). Exploitation: One view of industry and business. *Journal of Industrial Teacher Education, 25*(1), 12–22.

Swanson, R. A., & Sleezer, C. M. (1987). Training effectiveness evaluation. *Journal of European Industrial Training, 11*(4), 7–16.

Swanson, R. A., & Sleezer, C. M. (1988a). Determining financial benefits of an organization development program. *Performance Improvement Quarterly, 2*(1), 55–65.

Swanson, R. A., & Sleezer, C. M. (1988b). Organizational development: What's it worth? *Organizational Development Journal, 6*(1), 37–42.

Swanson, R. A., & Sleezer, C. M. (1989). Measurement practice meets measurement science. In C. M. Sleezer (Ed.), *Improving human resource development through measurement* (pp. 1–4). Alexandria, VA: American Society for Training and Development Press.

Tichy, N. M. (1983). *Managing strategic change.* New York: Wiley.

Torraco, R. J. (1992). Accelerated training 1992: Buyer beware. *Human Resource Development Quarterly, 3*(2), 183–186.

Torraco, R. J., & Swanson, R. A. (1991). *Auditing the strategic alignment of quality improvement, organization development, and training programs to the business.* St. Paul: Training and Development Research Center, University of Minnesota.

Tribus, M. (1985). *Becoming competitive by building the quality company.* Kingsport, TN: American Quality and Productivity Institute.

von Bertalanffy, L. (1968). *General systems theory: Foundations, development, applications.* New York: Braziller.

Wheatley, M. J. (1992). *Leadership and the new science: Learning about organization from an orderly universe.* San Francisco: Berrett-Koehler.

Yin, R. K. (1993). *Applications of case study research.* Newbury Park, CA: Sage.

Zemke, R., & Kramlinger, T. (1982). *Figuring things out: A trainer's guide to needs and task analysis.* Reading, MA: Addison-Wesley.

Index

T

V

W

Z

The Author

Richard A. Swanson is professor and director of the Human Resource Development Center at the University of Minnesota and senior partner of Swanson & Associates, Incorporated. He earned his B.A. and M.A. degrees in industrial education from Trenton State College and his Ed.D., also in industrial education, from the University of Illinois.

Swanson has received numerous awards, including the American Society for Training and Development national award for outstanding contribution to the academic advancement of human resource development, the Outstanding Trainer of Trainers Award from the Minnesota Chapter of the American Society for Training and Development, the G. Harold Silvius Outstanding Scholarly Publication Award, and the Bowling Green State University Faculty Research Award. He is the founding editor of the *Human Resource Development Quarterly* and has served as editor of the *Journal of Industrial Teacher Education* and the *Performance and Instruction Journal*.

Before joining the University of Minnesota faculty in 1979, Swanson was professor and coordinator of graduate studies in industrial technology at the University of Northern Iowa and professor and director of graduate studies in career and technology education at Bowling Green State University. With Deane Gradous he has coauthored *Performance at Work* (1986) and *Forecasting Financial Benefits of Human Resource Development* (1988). His coedited books include *Adapting Human Resources to Organizational Change* (with Gradous, 1987), *Performance Appraisal: Perspective on a Quality Management Approach* (with McLean and Damme, 1990), and *Innovative Meeting Management* (with Knapp, 1991). In addition, he is author of more than 150 publications on the topic of education for work.

During Swanson's twenty-five years of experience, he has consulted for several of the largest corporations in the United States in the areas of strategic human resource planning, personnel training, organization development, and quality improvement. He recently completed trips to Japan and Germany for the purpose of studying their quality improvement, organization development, and training practices. Swanson is currently doing research on education and training for organization, process, and individual performance improvement.